THE MAKER'S GUIDE TO MAGIC

ALSO BY ANDREA HANNAH

YOUNG ADULT
Where Darkness Blooms

THE
MAKER'S
GUIDE TO
MAGIC

How to Unlock Your Creativity
Using Astrology, Tarot, and Other Oracles

ANDREA HANNAH

ST. MARTIN'S
ESSENTIALS
NEW YORK

First published in the United States by St. Martin's Essentials,
an imprint of St. Martin's Publishing Group

www.stmartins.com

Designed by Steven Seighman

Illustrations by Rhys Davies

Library of Congress Cataloging-in-Publication Data

Names: Hannah, Andrea, author.
Title: The maker's guide to magic : how to unlock your creativity
   using astrology, tarot, and other oracles / Andrea Hannah.
Description: First Edition. | New York : St. Martin's Essentials, 2023.
Identifiers: LCCN 2023016826 | ISBN 9781250859747 (trade
   paperback) | ISBN 9781250859754 (ebook)
Subjects: LCSH: Magic. | Creative ability. | Tarot. | Oracles. |
   Astrology.
Classification: LCC BF1595 .H366 2023 | DDC 133.4/3—dc23/
   eng/20230509
LC record available at https://lccn.loc.gov/2023016826

Our books may be purchased in bulk for promotional, educational, or business use. Please contact your local bookseller or the Macmillan Corporate and Premium Sales Department at 1-800-221-7945, extension 5442, or by email at MacmillanSpecialMarkets@macmillan.com.

First Edition: 2023

10 9 8 7 6 5 4 3 2 1

CONTENTS

PART III. THE PROCESS

*For all the students, clients, and friends who have
entrusted me with their dreams.
I'm in awe of your magic.*

INTRODUCTION

As I'm writing this, there's a candle burning on my desk. An aura quartz carved into the shape of a unicorn is tucked in beside my keyboard, and my favorite tarot deck sits beside yesterday's empty coffee mug. My entire work space is a snowfall of crystals and cards, smoky incense sticks and mala beads. And yet, none of these things makes creative magic happen.

All of these items are tools I'm currently in communion with while I write. They're helpers, in a way—reminding me of the high standards I set for myself and my work, my wishes and wants, and the goals I carefully craft at the beginning of every project. But in truth, I've experienced potent, world-shifting magic while I've been sitting in a maple tree. Staring out a snowy window. Eating a plateful of pasta. Watering a wilting plant.

I've even experienced magic when my life has fallen apart around me.

I know that this is the part where I'm supposed to tell you how I came into this work and how, exactly, my life came undone at the seams and magic helped me stitch it back together. That's what usually comes next in these types of books, right? A testimonial of sorts. Proof that I know how this whole thing works.

I'm not going to do that here.

No one needs to relive trauma to prove a point to anyone, but especially not within a vacuumed space to people who haven't asked to hold it. Instead, I'll tell you this: I've seen some shit. Just like you have. Like we all have.

There's no way to live in this tumultuous day and age without having experienced some form of life-altering heartbreak. This is a weird time to exist, to try to make art that feels good and a life that feels even better when the very foundation we've built modern society on is crumbling. When what you've always known in your bones is no longer certain, everything feels shaky. The cracks show sooner. Other people will break your heart—but, love, you've probably broken your own heart, too. That's just what it's like to be a person with creative inklings in this wild time we're living in. Between the looming climate crisis, a breakdown of human rights, and a culture of urgency and immediacy, it's a constant struggle to listen to the whispers of our nudges, our urges, and the longing to express ourselves while trying to protect whatever safe space we have.

Breaking our own hearts can look like working a soul-sucking job to survive. It's watching our writing time slip through our fingers as friends and family and dependents poke holes in our plans. It's following through on the responsibilities over the art, the laundry over the longing.

All this to say: It's impossible *not* to break your own heart.

Kids gotta eat. The car needs an oil change. You need clean underwear.

This world wasn't made for people like you and me. It's not a soft place or a safe place, and it has sharp edges that cut deep. Everyone wants more art—more media, more entertainment, more pieces that remind us of what it means to be human—but no one wants to pay for it, with money or time or space. Sure, you can write your "little stories," but you'll have to do it in the dankness of the break room during your thirty-minute lunch. You need a studio, you say? A wobbly card table tucked into the corner of the garage is all you get. And forget about paying you for that art— we're going to give you "exposure."

The expectation on creatives to produce without the softness and support they need used to make my blood boil, so much so that I actively revolted against the idea for a while. If no one was going to offer me the bare essentials to create, then I just wouldn't create at all.

According to my friends, family, and therapist, that did not go well for me. Maybe you've come to the same conclusion, too. For a lot of us, not making art isn't an option for a variety of reasons, including our own mental health.

I moved on to step two: I would take up *more* space than needed. I would make a power grab for it with the same audacity of a mediocre dude in middle management. I would plant my flag in the middle of my home and protect my old oak desk with a feral gnashing of teeth.

It felt *good.*

It also didn't work.

Something happens to your creativity when you harden

your heart like that. I'm not talking about healthy, essential boundaries—those are key to thriving. I'm talking about the crust that forms around your heart when you're consistently furious and on guard. It cakes on so thickly that you're unable to feel the pulse and rhythm of your creation. It also takes all the joy out of it.

So here's the kicker: We live in a shaky world that doesn't value or even understand the creative process. We can't *not* make art, and we corrode our hearts when we get vicious about the process. Where does that leave us?

At a once-in-a-lifetime threshold, love.

Pain is where the light gets in. We know that. And we've been collectively dealing with the pain of being so deeply misunderstood for hundreds, if not thousands, of years. Of trying to fit in and build a life in the cracks of a society that was never set up with us in mind. But things aren't as set in stone as they were even two years ago, and people are getting tired of systems and structures that just don't work. There's an opening, a gap between No Longer and Not Yet, and we have the opportunity to plant something lush and vibrant here. Something that will nourish all the future creatives that come after us.

This is how we access the magic to create.

Magic is a tender thing, felt most often in the agony of a sleepless night and the lull between scattered thoughts. There's a reason why witches live at the edges of society—it's quiet enough there to hear its whispers in the raw potential waiting for us.

We're in an era where creatives have to live and work in

the throes of society. And, I suspect, there are more of us now than there have ever been, even if we don't quite know it yet. We *are* the middle management now, though we're anything but mediocre.

In this new age, we get to choose from a place of power instead of fear. We get to go spelunking in our minds until we unearth the nuggets of wisdom that remind us how to take care of ourselves, how to engage with our creativity again. Some days, that may look like shoving a sandwich in your mouth while typing up a few sentences on your phone. Some days, that may look like carefully placed crystals and an in-depth ritual.

The point is that you get to choose how you do it.

For you.

For all of us.

BUT SERIOUSLY, AM I CREATIVE ENOUGH FOR THIS BOOK?

Short answer: Absolutely. One hundred percent, no questions asked.

Long answer: As a society, we've put a lot of pressure on artists, writers, musicians, and other creatives to be certain kinds of people, to see the world a certain way, and to commodify their work. That's been painful for *everyone,* for different reasons.

First, the so-called creatives. By placing such heavy (and honestly, really weird) expectations on people who make art for a living or as a part of their everyday lives, we've boxed in the type of people we think can be called *creative*. Maybe you've heard of some of these tropes before, but here are a few I've come across as a working writer:

✦ *You must love to sit around and daydream all day.*
✦ *You must be very sensitive.*
✦ *You must have some deep trauma you want to get out and share with the world.*
✦ *You writers just operate differently from the rest of us.*

And those are the pretty innocuous ones. Let's not even go into the old-school stereotypes about writers and artists as utterly broke, unstable humans incapable of feeding themselves or otherwise existing in the physical world. All this performative drama on what it means to be a "creative" has left a lot of people confused and slightly terrified. I mean, why would anyone want to make art as a part of their regular lives if it means you can't have any friends and you have to be completely separated from reality?

On the other side of that, we have an entire generation of people who think that they aren't creative at all because they don't fit those tropes. They think that because they like to paint houses instead of canvases, or make meals instead of music, they don't have a creative bone in their body. And that is just not true.

I've spent thousands of hours teaching about writing, astrology, creativity, and wellness. I've taught everywhere from Google's offices to art studios to college campuses, and I can honestly say that I have never come across someone who could *not* create. Maybe they hadn't yet acquired the skills they needed to be able to make what's in their imagination, or maybe they didn't feel confident enough to follow their creative passions in earnest, but every single person was able to make *something*. And that, at its core, is what it means to be a creative. You are someone who makes something.

Preparing a delicious meal for your family qualifies as being a creative. So does building a birdhouse, starting a business, launching a product, and planning the company picnic. Whether you're making lesson plans, butter noodles, space in your closet, or a cross-stitched curse word, it's all valid, and it's all on an equal playing field. Seriously. I mean that. What you create is of no lesser value than what anyone else creates in this world. The sooner you come to accept that, the sooner you can take yourself as a creative seriously while opening up more space in your life for your projects.

Throughout this book, I'll use the word *creative* often, but please know that I am always, always talking about you. No matter who you are, how old you are, where you come from, or what you make. Your creativity and mine are in a symbiotic relationship; when you create, the magic you tap into spreads into the world, fueling the dream for even more of us. We are all working partners in this journey to higher creativity.

That's why you're here in the first place, I imagine. Maybe you picked out this book on a shelf or you saw it online, or maybe someone gave you their copy and told you to read it. Somehow this little book about magic and creativity found its way to you, and you're here now, trying to figure out if it is going to do anything for you. Please know this: You *are* creative in more ways than you can even imagine, and there is something that longs to be made *through you.*

We all have at least one thing that longs to be made through us. It whispers at the edge of our consciousness before we fall asleep. It gives us hints throughout our lifetimes, lighting us up with a warm glow from the inside whenever we see something that reminds us of the possibilities. It's the answer to our what-if questions that linger like persistent ghosts in the back of our minds.

Maybe you know exactly what you want to create, and you're looking for a way to bring even more power and potential to your work. You're in the right place. Or maybe you feel stuck in your creative life and are looking for a fresh approach to accessing this part of yourself. You are *also* in the right place. Maybe you have no idea what you want to make at all and you're not quite sure how you feel about astrology, tarot, and other sacred arts. Yep, still in the right place.

As far as I can tell from teaching and working closely with people of all walks of life for over a decade, we all have at least one thing we want to bring forth in the world. (There's even evidence of this in our astrological charts, but more on that later.) And by knowing yourself and your process, you can tap into your highest, most powerful magical self to make what you long to create. It may take a bit of flexibility, a dash of bravery, and a whole lot of dedication, but you are absolutely creative enough for this book, this mission.

That I can promise you.

EMBRACE YOUR INNER WITCH. OR UNICORN. WHATEVER WORKS.

For many of us, the last time we got up close and personal with magic was when we were kids. We devoured tales about wizards and talking animals, believed in monsters under our beds and gnomes in the garden, and even chased flickers of light across the walls in hopes we would catch a fairy. Once our childhood versions of magic faded, our preoccupation with it did, too, and we haven't looked back since.

In truth, magic never stopped existing; we were just expected to stop believing in it. I'll go into the definition of magic and how it relates to creativity in the next chapter, but first, we need to allow our preconceived notions to soften a bit before we move forward. It's the only way we can fully absorb what magic has to teach (and reteach) us.

Right about now, the cynics among us may be saying, "Well, yeah, I believed that everything was magical when I was five because I didn't know how science worked." And yes, that's true, but let me blow your mind a little here: *You can believe in magic and science at the same time.*

We tend to forget that science is not an absolute. Science, at its core, is the method of discovering what *might* be true through experiments that can be replicated based on the hypothesis posed with all of the knowledge we've collected up until *right now*. The key word there is *method*; we are constantly learning and unlearning, finding answers and then promptly discarding them. Science is an active process, one that will never be fully "done." In fact, there are plenty of "magical" practices that paved the way for scientific discovery. Alchemy, for example, was a medieval practice and philosophy that used magic for transformation of matter. It was our precursor to chemistry, which explains how and why different forms of matter interact with each other. And let's not forget ancient herbalism and potion-making. We can thank those witchy practices for paving the way for modern medicine.

The point is, there are plenty of phenomena that human beings once considered magical until science explained how they work. And for as long as we occupy the planet, and continue to grow and evolve, that demystification will never stop happening. We will continue to surprise ourselves, if we're lucky.

To me, magic is part of the phenomena that we don't quite understand yet. It's a step further than our logical minds and technology will take us. But just because we can't see how the pieces fit together *yet,* that doesn't make the experience any less meaningful or powerful. And it surely doesn't mean that something doesn't *work.* We just don't know how it does, for now.

I like to think that maybe our childhood selves could sense that there was just a little more than what we already know, only slightly out of reach. Like canaries in a coal mine, the curious, open-minded kid version of ourselves could sense that there is more out there than what the adults in our lives decided. That our squishy, underdeveloped brains still had the plasticity to consider seemingly wild possibilities and that our hearts had not calcified so much that we couldn't pursue something for no other reason than just to see what happens.

Let's try to go back there, to this place of childhood wonder and curiosity, for a second. It was that same sense of profound wonder that drew you to magic—or at least made you a little bit curious about it. Allow yourself to embrace your inner witch as you read through the rest of this book. Or, if you aren't ready to go full-on forest witch with a house full of tinctures and star charts, consider another magical being or archetype you were drawn to as a child. Embrace the part of you that once loved unicorns, fairies, magicians, superheroes, mermaids, or something entirely of your imagination. Give yourself the space to consider that the ancient, magical tools in this book may one day be the subject of a scientific discovery.

To do this, all you'll need is a trusty journal, notebook, or grimoire. I've set up *The Maker's Guide to Magic* to allow you to complete the exercises in real time, as you're reading through the book, so that you'll end up with a full ritual or method you can do to center yourself before you start your work, and a whole bunch of tools and strategies to use when you need a creativity boost. While I love a guide filled with activities that push me to get outdoors, collect resources, and spend time outside of my reading experience, I also know that I'm way more likely to skip past an activity that requires me to, you know, actually get off the couch. Even if I have the good intention to go back and do it later, I oftentimes never get back around to it. All you have to do is grab a pen and paper, and keep it close by so you can record the magic as it happens.

AN INTENTION AND A PROMISE

To start, I'll introduce (or reintroduce) you to concepts with which you probably already have some sort of relationship. I'll lay out my definitions for these concepts, but by the end of this book, I hope that you'll be able to layer in your own meaning to each one. Creating new things and the process by which you do so is deeply personal; it makes sense that the foundation of this work lies in your unique relationship to these concepts.

So let's break out your new grimoire before we head into the next section, shall we? Open up to a fresh page and write down the following words, giving yourself plenty of space between each one:

Magic
Creativity
Creative
Activation
Tool

Together, we'll explore the meaning of each of these words. As you go through part 1, let these reimagined definitions marinate in your mind. You can jot down my definitions if they resonate with you. Otherwise, feel free to choose the parts that *do* resonate, build your own definition from those seeds, and leave the rest behind.

My intention for this guide is that you turn to the last page feeling seen, whole, and unapologetic about taking up space in the world, as a human and a creative. You'll walk away from the text with a clearer understanding of yourself, as well as a toolbox full of tools that resonate with you and the know-how to use them, whether you're just beginning a project or you've gotten stuck somewhere along the way.

My promise is that if you do the deep work of reimagining your foundation, developing new methods, and opening your heart and mind to fresh possibilities, you'll get there. I know you will, and I'll be with you every step of the way.

PART I

THE MAGIC OF MAKING

1

WHAT *IS* MAGIC, ANYWAY?

THE FIRST TIME I touched magic, I was seven years old. There was a Japanese maple tree outside of my aunt and uncle's home, and I used to admire the gem-toned leaves whenever I visited. I'd reach up my hand and tuck a velvety leaf into my fist as I approached the porch. Sometimes, I'd pluck it and put it into my backpack, or press it between the pages of a library book, where it would inevitably stain the text a muted red.

I wish I could tell you that something truly out of this world happened, but it didn't. It would make for an interesting story, wouldn't it? That I went to pluck a leaf from my nature bestie and the tree said something like, "What's up, friend? Can you *not*?" But unfortunately for us all, that did not occur.

Here's what did occur.

After hanging out near this particular tree five days a week, I started to notice how it felt to *not* be in this tree. Almost as soon as my sneakers hit the soil, I'd get tired, like my battery had come unplugged from a power source. Then I started to notice how I'd get that excited, tingly feeling in my stomach when the school bus tires squealed to a stop every weekday afternoon. That sound meant I was only a few minutes away from scaling that tree.

Magic is tricky like that. Sometimes, you notice what the absence of it feels like before you recognize the living, breathing miracle. They say that you don't recognize the best years of your life while you're in them, and I think that's true for magic, too.

One goal of this book is to learn to feel it while it's happening so that you can identify everything that's not it. This way, you'll know in your bones when you're in flow with creative magic—or when you're creating at your highest potential possible—and when you're not. And you'll be able to identify which tools help to amplify your own personal brand of magic, loud and clear, so you can't miss it.

* * *

There have been a lot of definitions for magic throughout human history, all with varying degrees of reliance on the supernatural. One thing is consistent, though: The concept of magic has been present in every culture in some way, shape, or form.

Greco-Roman traditions wrote of magi who possessed secret, or arcane, knowledge. The Celts spoke (and still speak) of the power of the natural world. African shamans possess an extraordinary amount of knowledge in order to heal others from the inside out. Even the Wise Men of Holy

Bible infamy were considered extremely knowledgeable astrologers who proved the cosmic significance of Jesus's birth.

Definitions of magic differ across cultures, but most eventually land on magic as the active manipulation of an unseen force of some kind. Here's *Merriam-Webster*'s definition, for example:

magic /'ma-jik/ (n.): the power of apparently influencing the course of events by using mysterious or supernatural forces.

Personally, I think this definition is missing something. Yes, magic as we've come to know it as a modern society references the ability to wield unseen power to our liking, but there is a much deeper level to it that has nothing to do with what we crave or long for. It's also about what the universe wants for *us*.

James Joyce invented a term for this push-pull between internal and external forces. He called it "chaosmos," or a blend of *cosmos* (ordered structure) and *chaos*. Too much order will leave us feeling stale and uninspired. Too much chaos will keep us from ever reaching our full potential. Similarly, true magic requires a balance of cosmos and chaos to work to our highest advantage.

Let's think of it this way: We, as humans, are chaos beings. I don't care if you're the most even-keeled being on the planet, who eats plain oatmeal for breakfast every day of your life and will continue to do so until you die: You are a chaos being. You're *meant* to be a chaos being. We're on a spinning rock in the sky that is filled with man-eating crocodiles and volcanic eruptions and treacherous heart-breaks and internet trolls. I would be concerned if you were not feeling something—and sometimes acting on it. It's the Wild West down here, and no one's bothered to pave the roads.

You're the chaos in this "chaosmos" equation.

And whatever power you believe in—devas, elements, god(dess), planets, spirit guides, your subconscious—is the cosmos. Typically, the key difference between someone who believes in an outside force and someone who doesn't is their diverging views on randomness. To a nonbeliever, life is composed of random events that have no structure or order. But if you're someone who believes in *something*, even if you aren't sure exactly what that something is, then you also believe in some kind of order to the universe—a reason things happen the way they do, even if you don't agree with or completely understand them.

It doesn't matter if you haven't quite figured out what that "power" is that you believe in. It could be the Force, negentropy, David Bowie, aliens, or a man sitting on a cloud throne in the sky—for the purpose of making magic, all you need to do is believe that there's something else out there. That brings us to my definition of magic, tweaked to include you, me, and the universe:

magic /'ma-jik/ (n.): a conversation between the cos-mos and the human heart.

Working with magic isn't about control—although there are certainly plenty of people throughout history who have gotten caught up in that sort of thing. At its purest, magic is simply a heartfelt conversation between the divine order of the universe and the raw wanting of your very human heart, and you can access what is being said at any time. It's spoken in whispers, though, as the cosmos works to soothe your heart, telling it that it's okay to let go a little, to surrender a little, to *let me help you through this.*

And your feral heart replies, "Just let it feel like the truth."

THE RELATIONSHIP BETWEEN CREATIVITY AND MAGIC

Artists and philosophers have been trying to put words to that spark of inspiration that sets us afire for centuries. Plato insisted that the Muses inspire us, while Nietzsche believed that the greatest creative feats were born from a collaboration between the spirits of passion and restraint. Aristotle, Socrates, and Kant all gave it a shot, too, and yet we're still trying to put words to it today. In *Big Magic,* author Elizabeth Gilbert writes, "I believe that creativity is a force of enchantment—not entirely human in its origins."

There are a lot of similarities between magic and creativity. Both have to do with some sort of unseen inspiration or influence. Both require you to take a peek around your heart to consider what's important to you, the tiny wishes and wants you'd like to make manifest.

And here's the secret that authors and artists, philosophers and shamans, have been bumping against all this time: Magic and creativity are one and the same.

There's a reason why the Aramaic phrase *avra kehdabra* has stood the test of time. It's changed over thousands of years, but it's still a part of our modern-day vernacular, only now we know it as *abracadabra*. It's the arcane word that magicians use to work with the supernatural.

Avra kehdabra, or abracadabra, translates to "I will create as I speak."

Magic and creativity are inextricably linked. When you are creating something—*anything*—you are working with magic. Your heart and the universe are in deep conversation, and you are the mediator standing between them, considering both sides. Whatever collaboration these two decide on is made by *you*. Your experiences, beliefs, preferences, gifts, and talents are the filters that determine which shape and form this collaboration will take. Your hopes and fears dictate who you'll share it with.

This is exactly why it's so important to get to know and consciously amplify your magic. Imagine what it would feel like to sit down at your work space every day and feel magic coursing through you, to trust that you're creating from the most powerful version of yourself. Imagine closing your paint kit or laptop at the end of the day and feeling a deep sense of peace and satisfaction about the work you did. And even better: having the tools and know-how to bring yourself to that state of creative bliss again tomorrow, and the next day, and the next.

If magic is a unique conversation with your heart and the universe, creativity is what you do with the wisdom you glean from that conversation. To be clear: Magic is always at play here, even if you aren't consciously aware of it. Some things you make may only have an echo of magic, while others may be positively riddled with it. The latter are the creations that feel wholly *you*. They challenge you, but in a fruitful way that feels both exciting and soothing at the same time. These are the projects you finish and know in your heart that you were made to create *exactly this*. There's no better feeling, and there's never been a time in my life where I've been more reverent: of my work, my process, and my life.

When you get to know your magic, including how it presents itself to you and ways to identify and access it regularly, you begin to create things on a whole new level. Suddenly, your work sings at a higher octave, and it seems like the universe is cheering you on the whole way through, often providing you with exactly what you needed at the most perfect time. And most important, you get to settle into the feeling that you know you are making what you were meant to make with no regrets or what-ifs.

Ready to begin?

Let's start this journey of getting to know your magic on a personal level.

IDENTIFYING YOUR MAGIC

I have never been the kind of magic-maker who can float up to the astral plane at will or hear their ancestors whisper to them through the creaky floorboards of their childhood home. I'm a tactile, gritty kind of human who relies on my senses to suss out magic. With a lot of practice, I've eventually gotten to the point where I can recognize when magic is happening *while it's happening* instead of after I've already unplugged from it.

For me, it all comes down to what it feels like.

Just like you've learned to identify what joy and heartbreak feel like based on your life experiences, you can also learn to identify what it feels like when you brush up against magic. The thing that makes this a little trickier than sussing out universal emotions like melancholy and elation is that magic will feel different to everyone. There's a kind of collective blueprint for common emotions—depression is a heaviness, while happiness is a bubbly effervescence—but we haven't drawn out that map for magic. Add to that our unique individual strengths and weaknesses and how quietly magic tends to whisper, and it's downright challenging to figure out what it feels like.

Discovering your own unique brand of magic and how to identify it is going to involve two paths: the path of destruction and the path of creation. To give our magic a fair chance at connecting with us, we first must blow up our preconceived notions about it—even the ones we didn't know we had. And I guarantee we all have them.

Even now, I still catch myself thinking it should be something more flamboyant than my personal brand of magic is. I grew up in the Catholic Church, where any talk of witchcraft and magic-wielding was an obvious no-no, as the source of our power was supposed to come from the Big Man in the sky. And even though I've cleared a lot of that, I still find myself wondering if what I'm feeling is really magic or if maybe I'm being a little narcissistic in thinking that

I'm worthy enough to be in conversation with something so powerful.

All this to say, it's extremely important to actively identify and break down our preconceived ideas around magic. It's a lifelong process, but the more you hack away at it with your magic machete, the easier it gets.

It's also important to then *consciously make your own blueprint of magic.* This is where you get to identify what magic feels like to you, as well as set the framework for how you can most easily access it. The universe abhors a vacuum, and if you go around chopping down old belief systems, you should be sure to plant the seeds of what you want to grow in their place. Otherwise, you may not like what's planted there for you.

So how do we do that? Let's start with a little destruction.

SPELLWORK: SCRATCH IT OUT

As creatives, we already know there's power in words. In this exercise, we're going to use the power of the pen to scratch out the words that no longer serve us.

Open your notebook, journal, or grimoire to a fresh page. You'll want to put the date at the top so you can go back and see how much you've grown and changed over the course of reading this book and beyond. Start by deciding how long you'll write for. Some magic-makers may want to fill up an entire page, or two, or three. Others may want to write for five minutes or longer. Whatever you land on, just be sure that it feels like a little bit *too* much. It should be just a bit uncomfortable.

Then, start ruminating on the concept of "magic." The worst thing you can do here is overthink this. Just write everything that comes to mind, continuously, until you've reached the mark you set for yourself. I promise you that not everything you write will be profound; in fact, a lot of it probably won't. I've written some of the most out-there and inane stuff of my life during these types of exercises, and a lot of it never ended up meaning anything. This is *okay*. It's just the dust settling as your brain works over the task at hand, and it's completely normal.

When you're finished, close your eyes for a minute and take a deep breath that fills up your entire belly, then release it through your mouth (say hello to the ujjayi breath—one of yoga's greatest tools, which we'll talk about more in this book). Open your eyes and take a look at what you wrote.

Really take in all of it—the nonsense and the gibberish, the profound and the profane. Then, when you're ready, take that same pen and start scratching out anything on the page that you no longer want to hold on to when it comes to your beliefs surrounding magic.

Maybe you were raised in a strict religious household, and you learned that magic was an act of evil. Maybe the only experience you have with magic is in novels and movies. Maybe you wrote a whole lot of nonsensical sentences that sound some-thing like, "MAGIC MAGIC MAGIIIICCC." All of that is valid, that last one included.

Even if you know nothing at all about magic, consider *not* bringing that sense of confusion into your new experience of working with it. You want to be knowledgeable and confident and focused. You want to feel empowered in your creative practice, and like *you've got this.* Any sentence—any *word*—that doesn't align with that vision, scratch it out.

Finally, take a look at what's left. Maybe there's a lot left on the page, or maybe there's nothing at all. Whatever is left or not left is perfect the way it is.

You can end this exercise here and keep reading; the power of this practice is in the intention you set over anything else. But if you're feeling like you want to take it a step further and really banish these un-inspired thoughts, burning this sheet of paper (in a fire-safe container, of course) is a great way to really release this. Then, pour the ashes into garden soil or down the drain.

MAKING WITH MAGIC

Now that you've said goodbye to your preconceived notions, there's a lot of open space to fill with fresh ideas around magic. That's exactly the imagery we're going to tap into for this next section.

I've had students and clients ask me over the years why I use the word *creative* instead of *creator,* especially when I teach magic and creativity as a method of empowerment. It seems like *creator* would be more active, like we're the ones in control, whereas *creative* sounds more passive, as if we aren't in control of the process at all.

The truth is: They're right. *Creative is* a more passive term than *creator,* and yet, I consciously chose it. To me, the passive form of the word is a humbling of sorts. It requires us to recognize that making things means we are inspired or filled up with whatever unique power we believe in. It's a process of surrender, and a deep recognition that we, actually, are not fully in charge. In my opinion, that's a good thing! If it's not all on us to write the next Great American Novel, paint the next *Starry Night,* or perform the lead in the next *Hamilton,* that means we can reach out for help when we need it—from friends, family, community, and yes, magic.

Let's vibe with that for a minute. Think of being a creative as being a vessel or toolbox that you can fill with inspiration, tools, strategies, activations, insights, unicorns—whatever you'd like. Take that in for a minute: *You* can fill yourself up. To start, we're going to tap into deep-seated wisdom and bring forth some insights that you can use to identify your magic.

And the best part? Once you can identify it, you can draw from it anytime you want or need. To me, that sounds so much more appealing than creating out of sheer grit and unavoidable burnout.

So let's do that. Now that we've made some room, we can dive into what we *do* want to consciously place in our creative vessel, starting with the unique texture of our magic.

• •

SPELLWORK: THE TEXTURE OF MAGIC

You'll need your trusty notebook again for this one. First, turn to a fresh page and write the date at the top. In the center, draw a "vessel." Maybe you're someone who aligns with the idea of an upside-down triangle (the symbol of the divine feminine) or a circle (a symbol for wholeness and truth). Or maybe you'd rather just draw a square to represent a strong container. The only requirement is that you make it large enough to fill up most of the page.

Then take a minute to pause and breathe. When was the last time you felt really on fire with something, whether it was while taking a yoga class or strumming a guitar? When were you most recently "in the zone"? If you can't recall a specific event, try to think of big-picture patterns. When are you *most likely* to feel in flow?

Take a second to relive that moment or moments. If you had to describe what your personal brand of magic felt like then in three words, which descriptors would you use? For me, my magic always feels like tiny, effervescent bubbles that start in my hands, usually because I feel it most often when I'm typing away at my keyboard. Other creatives I've worked with have experienced their flow, or magic, by the blood rushing to their cheeks or when their stomach hitches to let them know they're on the right track. There's no wrong answer here.

Now, zoom in on the moment or moments a little closer. What scent was wafting in the air? What colors or objects stood out to you? What was beneath your feet—a petal-soft blanket, spindly weeds, something else entirely? Really take your time to absorb the textures that were surrounding you in that experience.

Maybe you noticed that you always seem to be outdoors when you're really tapping into flow, or maybe you're always wearing the same soft blue sweater. Our five physical senses help to ground us in our experiences, and drawing on them can help to remind our nervous system that *we've done this before* and we can do it again. We can put on that same soft blue sweater and sit on the patio every time we create. We can experiment with time and place, texture and preferences, until we feel our magic while we're working. Then we can store those textures in our toolbox or vessel so we know how to activate our magic when we want to access it again.

Once you have a pretty good idea of some "textures" you can add to your page, go ahead and write about or draw them in your notebook. These are sacred tools to help you build a relationship with your personal brand of magic.

2

FOUR STEPS TO MAGIC

I THINK THE ancient Greeks were on to something when they started using the word *magike* in tandem with *teckné,* or the process of creating. When the two words appeared side by side, they denoted the process of making magic.

What's super interesting about this is the slightly muddled interpretation of *teckné.* It's difficult to assign a very specific meaning to it now, in modern society, because its connotation has changed over time, as language tends to do. To some, *teckné* represented the "lower-class" crafts by which people made with their hands. It also represented "higher" art further along in its evolution, but in general, the term refers to "making or doing."

My view on this is that *magike* is the mystical, ethereal part of making art, and *teckné* is the human part. *Teckné* is our 50 percent of the bargain that we need to deliver on. And since this word denotes that it's an actual, physical action or actions, it also means that we're going to have to put in some effort on our end to connect with it.

Ultimately, it makes sense, right? As much as I'd love for this book, or any of my books, to write itself, I have to show up at the desk every day to make it happen. I have to scribble out my notes, type and delete, type and delete, type and delete, delete, delete until I get it right. Even though there's magic to be made on the page, I still have to physically show up.

There are also steps that need to be taken to hear your own magic, loud and clear. Some of these things are simple actions that you can do right before you start to create, while others will take a little bit more time, effort, and energy to develop. All of them require you to take a step or two outside of your comfort zone as you absorb a new way of thinking about and working with your energy and creativity. Remember, the magic is in the process just as much as the product.

The Process

No matter which tools you decide to use to access your magic, there's a systematic process that you can use consistently, every time, before you work on a project. It doesn't matter if you're tucked into a cozy nest in your bed, working on your book, or drawing on your iPad on an airplane—you can still do all these steps.

It seems a little counterintuitive, doesn't it? When people think of creativity, they tend to envision this wide-open world with unlimited choices. They picture endless brain space and no restrictions, and this go-with-the-flow sense of letting inspiration come forth. But truly, some of our most vibrant ideas unearth themselves when we've applied boundaries to our work and lives. Even more important, order helps us to feel safe enough to actually pursue the project and see it through to completion.

If I asked you to find a way to exit a room but there were no rules or stipulations, you would most likely take the simplest way out: through the door. But if I told you to exit the room without using your hands, and you also can only touch every other tile on the floor, things get way more interesting. Boundaries help us think outside of the box.

As we now know, magic comes from the intersection of order and chaos. A process helps to put order in place so your subconscious can go to work churning up magic instead of overthinking the fine details or taking the easy way out. These are the four steps to the magic-making process to help you tap into yourself and your work. I'll go into each one in-depth in part 3, but for now, consider if and how you currently engage with each of these parts of the process. You may find that you do some version of one or all of these steps without even realizing.

1. CLEARING THE CHANNEL

Before you sit down to create, it's important to consider how you're feeling in that exact moment, address any blocks, and then clear the channel. Again, if you're the mediator between the universe and the longing of your heart, then *you* are the channel. You're the instrument by which your intuition speaks to you and the mechanism by which you can physically bring your idea to life, from the dream world to our world.

There's some responsibility in that role. You could show

up for your art as a grumpy, sluggish version of yourself, or you could show up for yourself first by ensuring you're calm and rejuvenated before you start. What you make is an extension of who you are in every single moment. That's why, a lot of times, authors cringe whenever they go back and read their own books. Sure, the craft wasn't as great as it is now (nor should it be), but the author themself has also changed from the blip in time when they wrote that story. It's like looking into a mirror and seeing someone you don't quite recognize anymore.

So why not set yourself up to be the truest version of you in this moment? That *you* is courageous and lionhearted, willing to be patient with themselves and seek out their own wisdom. They also know when it's time to look outside of themselves and tap their trusted community for advice, and how to check that advice against their own internal compass. This version of you—and we all have one of these, I swear—can create through even the wickedest storms. They're soft enough to feel it all but savvy enough to create strong boundaries.

Clearing the channel allows you to get to this version of you, in this moment, so that all the art you create is an expression of the connected and centered you. Whether you're making a quilt or business, you want your creation to come from this place. When you make from your sacred center, you also touch that part of your audience, reader, or consumer, in turn inspiring them to live and create from that place as well. Clarity increases your impact, and who wouldn't like to leave a positive imprint on the world by making heart-centered art? You'll learn how to use your new tools to clear your physical, mental, emotional, and spiritual bodies so you're ready to absorb all that your magic has to offer.

2. TUNING IN

As creatives, we all have something we want to say with our work in this world, but listening is just as important, if not more so. Listening to *what*? you may ask. The answer to that question is going to be different for everyone.

We've discussed how creativity and magic are intricately entwined, and this part of the process involves tuning in to an unseen force for more information before you dive in and start making. Whatever that unseen force is depends on your personal belief system. Maybe it's the divine order of the cosmos, like we discussed in the previous chapter. Or it could be a layer of your subconscious that you're finally unearthing, or your ancestors, or an archangel, or your grandpa that passed away in 1979. There are no wrong answers here, as long as you have one that makes sense to you.

The key is to decide who or what you're trying to connect with and then actively engage with it or them to build your relationship. Great partnerships must be built on the foundation of strong communication, and that includes listening as well as speaking. You'll want to get to know the source of your inspiration on a more personal level so that you know it like you know your best friend. You want to be able to distinguish this source from your own voice, to tell the difference between cosmic inspiration and your own anxieties. That way, the path toward making the kind of art you want to make becomes clearer, and you learn to lean into that intuition when you're feeling unmoored.

This is where a lot of people get stuck. They think that because they don't know for sure what or who they're tuning in to that they can't do so, or they block themselves from doing so, thinking that it's all in their imagination. Here's what I have to say to that:

So what?

Let's say you decide that you're talking to the ghost of Betty White (RIP, Betty), and every time you think that grandmotherly angel is giving you an intuitive nudge, you can't get over the idea that you're making it all up in your head. You know what? It's completely within the realm of possibility that you are making it up. It's also within the realm of possibility that you're *not*. But here's the thing: Even if you aren't sure if this is some fantasy of having Betty White as your fairy godmother playing out in your head or if she's actually there, whispering words of encouragement about your work in progress, it doesn't matter at this stage. What's most important is that you believe that something or someone outside of your physical flesh suit exists and that you can tap into it for help and encouragement whenever you need it.

As you learn how to tune in to this source of inspiration and build a stronger relationship with it, you'll also learn to clearly decipher it from your own wants, wishes, and longings. You'll learn how to set boundaries with your intuitive nudges, how to ensure that what you're perceiving is for the highest good of your art and yourself, and you'll gain more information about where your support and inspiration comes from. Who knows? Maybe you'll discover that it really was Betty White all along (and in that case, count me as extremely envious).

3. TAKING ACTION

Even if Betty White is your personal creativity coach, you still have to follow through on her words of wisdom to get things done. To make anything happen in this world, we have to meet the universe halfway. And splitting the difference with the universe is going to look different for each project you work on.

You may tune in to yourself, the universe, and your project and discover that you need to move in a totally new direction, and that means trashing that canvas you've spent months on. It may mean switching mediums, starting with a different color palette, deleting that Word doc, or telling your partner that you need a little more quiet time than usual to get the words on the page. Sometimes, meeting the universe halfway will be really hard, and it'll require time, sacrifice, and a whole lot of trust to get to the point where the magic starts happening.

Other times, it'll be as pleasant as a spring day. The magic may greet you as soon as you show up to sit at your computer, or pluck the strings on your guitar, or when you're thinking about your project late at night. The ideas and inspiration may feel like a flood instead of a steady trickle, so much so that you're trying not to drown in the force of your own creativity. Those are the fun times, the times when it's easy to trust that there's some source of cosmic intervention going on here. Enjoy those times, for sure, but remember that the real test is holding on to that sense of trust when things aren't going nearly as well.

No matter if it's hard or easy, taking what mystics and magic-makers throughout history call *aligned action* is the next step in making something that feels like you to the core. Sometimes, you may get the overwhelming urge to go grab a new set of ink pens. Other times, you may get the sense that you have to start over from scratch to make this project into what you truly want it to be. It's never easy, but you'll always be glad you did it.

4. Distilling the Wisdom

To most creatives, taking action until the work is complete is the final phase. They tend to think that just because the words are on the page and the paint is on the canvas that the magic-making is done for now.

But this is actually where the real work lies.

In yoga, an instructor will often lead a class through a series of intense postures, or asana. Then, there's a pause while you hold a pose, usually for several breaths. And then, of course, there's the big "pause" at the end of class where you lie down in Savasana, palms flipped up toward the ceiling, and simply rest. There's a reason for these intermediate pauses— they're essential to integration. Without a pause, or some kind of stillness and reflection period, it's extremely difficult to not only absorb knowledge but also integrate it into your daily life so you can put it to practical use before you start the next thing.

You only build muscle memory by allowing your body

to rest between workouts. You only remember new information you've read in a textbook when you allow your brain to cool down before you try to take the test. Anything that taxes your mental, physical, emotional, and spiritual muscles requires a "pause" period to help you distill all that you've learned down to its most potent essence. Every creative will unearth their own unique process for this task, but we *all* require the sacred pause to do so. From within this respite, whatever it looks like for you, you can begin to reflect on your project and process with a sense of wonder. It's from this inner reverence that we begin to knit together the information we've gathered along the way, weaving mismatched threads into something solid and useful that we can wrap ourselves in.

If anything, distilling the wisdom of what you've learned is the most critical magic-making strategy. Just like any exercise, craft, or skill, learning to work with the unseen forces of aligned, vibrant creativity is a lifelong endeavor that will include a lot of trial and error. Distilling the wisdom you learn along the way will help you to make the ride feel like an enticing experiment where you find yourself getting closer and closer to the heart of your truth each time you create instead of a labyrinth of dead ends. And *that's* where the magic happens.

* * *

While there are four steps to help you get from a brilliant idea to a finished product you can feel proud of, there are as many ways to work with the steps as there are people on the planet. That's really the most important thing to remember: The steps are the same for all of us, but there can be a world of difference between how one person gets through them compared to another.

There are a few guiding principles that I've had success with over the years, both personally and with students and clients. Keeping these principles in mind as you learn about the tools and oracles in this book will help you to decide which ones, if any, will work best for you.

SPELLWORK: FLIP THE SCRIPT

Take a close look at the four steps. Read over them again, then grab your trusty notebook. Which one of these four steps do you think you have the most difficulty with? Or if you aren't sure, which one do you feel most uncomfortable with at first glance?

Now let's flip the script. Ask yourself: *What knowledge do I need to feel totally comfortable with this step?*

For example, if you're feeling a little uncomfortable with the idea of clearing the channel, what tools, strategies, or concepts would you need to know to get really cozy with it? Maybe you'd need to know more about how to tell the difference between your intuitive guidance and fear, or if there are any physical tools, like a tarot deck, incense blend, or something else, that can help you out. Maybe you want to know more about how to understand yourself or how to even decide what message you want to send or art medium you want to work with. All valid. Write it all down.

Then, at the bottom of the page, write yourself a little note of encouragement. Maybe you had a parent who wrote those little love notes telling you, "Have a good day!" and left them in your lunchbox, or maybe you've dated someone who slipped you a note before a big day at work. Instead of waiting for someone else to tell you that you're going to figure it all out, that it's going to be okay, you're going to do that for yourself. If you're having trouble thinking of what you want to say, here are some options to get you started:

✦ *I have everything I need to discover my creative magic.*
✦ *Creativity is natural, and I know exactly how to access mine.*
✦ *It's easy to tap into my creative power.*
✦ *There's always a way to figure out what I need to know.*
✦ *I am magic.*

Research shows that it's incredibly difficult to learn anything new when we feel stressed and un-safe. Writing yourself a little love note affirming that you've got this can help to calm your nervous system so you can relax into this process with curiosity instead of anxiety.

Remember: You're the source of your own magic. And you've got this.

3

STARS, CARDS, AND COVENS

KNOWING THE STEPS to identify and work with your own magic is extremely important. I'll lead you through each of the steps in detail later in this book, but first, let's get to know the tools we're working with. Knowing which tools you vibe with is equally, if not more, important than the process. A pipe needs to be unobstructed for water to flow through it, but it doesn't really matter if you can't figure out how to open the valve. The tools you choose for working with your creative magic are how you turn the handle.

And let's be real: There are plenty of ways to turn on a faucet. Sure, most of us just reach for the handle and turn it to get the water flowing through the pipes, but that's not the only way to do it. You could push the knob with your elbow or your nose. You could grab an oven mitt or a pair of pliers and turn it on. You could even remove the handle altogether and let the water flow freely into the sink.

The point is this: It doesn't matter how you turn on the

water. What matters is that the method you choose resonates with you.

In this chapter, we'll go over some of the world's most ancient tools and languages. Things like astrology, tarot, and nature magic have been used by humans for thousands of years as methods of understanding ourselves and our place in the world, and they have a pretty good track record. As these tools have become more mainstream over the past few years, there's more information on the web and in books than there's ever been, which makes learning these tools a simpler process than in the past.

That said, if you'd rather use an oven mitt to turn on your faucet and I don't mention an oven mitt in these pages, by all means, go get yourself one. As I tell every student I work with, "Take what resonates with you and leave the rest behind." The same goes for this book. If you read through the chapters on astrology and you just can't get into them, no worries. If you try out some of the tarot spreads and you aren't feeling any closer to tapping into your magic, that's also okay. Sometimes, it takes multiple tries; and sometimes, you know right away that something isn't for you, at least not right now. Even if you do resonate with a tool as is, it's more than likely that you will begin to experiment with it, eventually modifying it according to your process, project, and purpose. We'll also discuss some other oracles, tools, and strategies you can explore, and we'll go over how to use pretty much *anything* as a tool for accessing magic.

Before we dive into that, let's lay down some groundwork for understanding the concepts that show up in this chapter and throughout the rest of this book.

TOOLS AND ACTIVATIONS

In the following paragraphs, I'll introduce you to some of the tools that ancients and mystics have worked with for centuries to access magic. But before we get there, there's another step between use of the tool and vibing with magic, and those are what I call *activations*. Here are my definitions of both.

> **TOOL:** *A concrete device or method that provides a pathway to an activation.*
> **ACTIVATION:** *A state of being that promotes alignment and synchronicity, from which we can more easily work with our magic.*

After working with creatives all over the world, both one-on-one and in large groups, it's become increasingly clear that our tender hearts are craving some similar states of being, or activations. At our core, we yearn to

✦ connect to the meaning and purpose of our work;
✦ create to our full potential; and
✦ be witnessed by and collaborate with like-minded individuals.

These three activations—connection, creativity, and collaboration—are the core of this book, but there are hundreds, if not thousands, of activations. Just to name a few: Ambition, wellness, alignment, and love are all activations, or states of being, that we can embody to get a little closer to our magic. And the tools that have been around for centuries—like yoga, astrology, tarot, oracles, meditation, and coven gatherings—have made it this far because they are capable of guiding us into a variety of activations. One person may find themselves building trust and honesty as they work with their tarot deck, while another may tap into a sense of community as they share their daily card pulls with others. These tools may work differently for us all, but they *work*. Period.

In the following sections, you'll find some starter information on astrology, tarot, and covens, as well as the three activations that tend to help creatives thrive. However, keep in mind that this is simply a guide; perhaps you'll get something different from stars, cards, and covens, and that is valid. This is just a map to help you move in the right direction. You get to decide how you're going to get there.

ASTROLOGY: CONNECTION IN THE STARS

Ancient mystics believed that there was infinite wisdom in the cosmos, and I wholeheartedly agree. I've never learned so much about myself than when I'm studying my birth chart, and as a professional astrologer, I've read thousands of other people's charts, too. Each person I've consulted with has told me that they gained new insights from a session—and that includes the biggest of skeptics.

Before you hop in here and mention that your ex was a two-faced Gemini and they're all terrible (as a Gemini, I object), let's be really clear: I'm not talking about pop astrology. I love a good zodiac meme just as much as the next modern mystic, but astrology as a language for understanding yourself is a *much* different thing from a Pisces crying over their wilted houseplants.

To the ancient Babylonians and Egyptians, fixed stars and transitory planets held deep meaning. And even before that, women drew the moon phases on cave walls to track their own menstrual cycles in time with this luminary's appearance in the sky. The planets and their movements have helped humans create order and connect the dots between personal development, world events, and what's happening in the sky above them.

This pattern-reading ability really comes in handy when you're trying to figure out how to make the things you've always dreamed of making. Astrology is a tool and a language, and it can give you the words you need to understand the connection between the mystical and the ordinary. And once you can see a connection between your inner life and outer events, you can work to actively leverage the strengths laid out in your chart and to create in sync with the cosmic weather. We can't change what we aren't aware of. Astrology gives us the opportunity to put words to our process so that we can actively use it to its fullest power and create with a lot less friction.

TAROT: CREATIVITY IN THE CARDS

Similarly, tarot has long-standing roots. The first official tarot decks on record showed up in the fifteenth century in Italy and have had a near-constant presence in a variety of spiritual practices ever since. In the past decade alone, the sales of tarot cards have boomed in North America, and there seems to be more talk of tarot on the internet than ever before.

What is it about the cards that has captured the imagination of people for centuries? Like astrology, tarot provides a modality to express a part of oneself. While the stars offer a way to access your connection to yourself, events, and others, tarot cards provide a tried-and-true tool for sparking creative solutions.

In a traditional Rider-Waite tarot deck, there are seventy-eight cards, split into the Major Arcana (twenty-two cards) and the Minor Arcana (fifty-six cards). The Major Arcana represents potent archetypes and themes like temperance and justice. The Minor Arcana includes four suits and represent different aspects of life, such as relationships, passion, finances, and strategic planning. All the cards feature rich imagery that catches the eye and sparks the imagination.

As tarot has exploded in popularity over the past few years, more and more decks have come out. There are a ton of fun and unique takes on tarot decks and a whole bunch of innovative oracle decks (more on the difference between the two later). Truly, there's something out there for everyone, and each guidebook has its own spin on what the cards mean. The key is to find a deck that works for you.

So how do you know if a deck is working for you? If it inspires a flicker of creativity, it's working. If it makes you see a problem or project from a different angle, it's working. If it makes you feel a little bit closer to the truth of your heart, it's definitely working.

A consistent tarot practice has helped me see plot problems from a totally new angle. It's taught me what my own intuition feels like, and most important, it's been a safe space to explore creative ideas. There have been more times than I can count when I've felt stuck with a project and I've pulled out my cards. At the right moment, the cards have shown me a brilliant way to patch up a plot hole, or what's gotten under my skin, or why I feel the way I do about someone's actions. Or more accurate, the cards have acted as a guide to point me toward the answers I already held within.

COVENS: COMMUNITY IN THE CIRCLE

The subtitle of this book is *How to Unlock Your Creativity Using Astrology, Tarot, and Other Oracles.* We've covered astrology and tarot, so you may be wondering when "other oracles" come in. We'll get into what constitutes an oracle in part 2. But first, I need to tell you more about covens.

I won't mince words: A trusted group of like-minded individuals is one of the most powerful tools—if not *the* most powerful tool—that exists. Not only can you safely learn about tarot and astrology in your group, but a space like this also gives you breathing room to explore other oracles, or even make your own.

Nothing is ever created in a vacuum. Even when you think you're creating alone, you're actually building upon the skills you've learned by studying others, from the traits and themes in a book character's lifetime, to your ancestors' wildest dreams for you in this lifetime. You are a constellation of all your circumstances and then some, and that is a beautiful thing.

We're told that creatives are lone wolves, that because we think and act differently and tend to exist in the fringes of society, that means we don't need other people. But the truth is that wolves are pack animals, and as my writer friend Kasey reminded me, wolves alone in the wild are usually *sick*. It's wholly unnatural for a wolf to take on the elements alone, and the same goes for humans, no matter our calling and purpose. We may not vibe with everyone, but we definitely need *someone*.

Just imagine what happens when you bring all of the sacred wisdom of *you* and combine it with the wisdom of others. There's a reason why witches gather in a circle and cast spells together, or why marginalized people have circled for centuries for ritual, and why communities gather for vigil and prayer. There is power in numbers. Individually, there's only so much we can do, so much energy we can generate. But collectively, we can topple dictatorships and change the course of history.

If that seems a little overdramatic, let's bring it back down to a smaller scale. How many times have you given up on something because there was no one to hold you accountable? Or to cheer you on? When you are part of a community, whether it's a climate change activist group, or an exercise studio, or a group of creatives that calls themselves a coven and meets a few times per month to talk about crystals and art shows, there's a natural sense of feeling held. Your coven holds space for you to explore, stumble, do the work, and you know they're cheering you on (and maybe even calling you out) while you go through it all.

THE SECRET ACTIVATION: POWER

Connection, creativity, and community are the foundation upon which we build a healthy, soulful creative life—the kind of life that's brimming with magic. And these tools and activations are just a handful of ways we can get there. At the end of the day, all paths—whether you walk these paths or find your own—are leading you toward your own power.

Power is a tricky concept. We're taught to be repulsed by it, shun it, and fear it. At the same time, we crave it. We wonder what it would be like to have it. Some of us dream about the kind of life we could have if we could share in even a sliver of it. But let me be clear about this: We can't claim power *and* abhor it. Not true power, anyway. Not the kind of power that changes the world through beautiful creations.

True power is nothing to be feared. Actually, it's something that we all have access to, that *we already possess* in spades. Our modern society with its emphasis on outward achievement at the cost of our soul, milquetoast relationships that never break through the surface, and industries that thrive on disconnecting us from our true source of power have warped our understanding of it. I don't think that was an accident. The less power we think we have, the easier it is to be controlled. To prevent us from saying no to conventional norms that keep us small. To stop us from making truly radical, world-changing things.

In our heart of hearts our true power lies, yearning for us to use it. When we can access it, we are unstoppable in our pursuit of and ability to cocreate with magic.

When we fully own our power, we are humbly standing at

the intersection of connection, creativity, and collaboration. From connection, we understand our specific place in this world—even within the cosmos—and how we can leverage our strengths, weaknesses, and the patterns in our lives to make something truly soul-changing. From creativity, we tap into our raw potential to stitch together a life full of meaning and magic. From collaboration, we are gifted the ability to unearth the hidden gems within ourselves we already have, all with the space and support to do so. Understanding and leaning into all three affords us to see our bigger place in the journey, the confidence to reach new horizons, and the support to hold us up. *That's* power.

Because of all the haze around the concept of power, it's tougher to, well, activate this activation. We have less (but not zero) collective baggage around concepts of connection, creativity, and community, so it's a bit easier for us to tap into the essence of those three on our mission to reclaim our power. When we work from this place, we access our magic with confidence and enthusiasm for the work ahead. Tuning out the negative voices and nonsense around us becomes so much easier because we feel whole just by creating. True power allows us to become stewards of creativity, wholly unto ourselves, and in direct contact with our magic.

As you learn new tools for accessing these activations and you explore each of them, you will build new pathways to your personal power. You'll grow stronger in your ability to create and make magic at the same time you're learning to do so.

Part of what gives politicians the audacity to run for public office without any experience, or CEOs the gall to give themselves a 200 percent raise, or for ancient alchemists to even attempt to make gold is that they *know* they can, even if the rest of us could make the argument that they're a little delusional.

It's time that creatives know, too. Who better to have access to power than the deep thinkers, the warmhearted, the intuitive, the ones tasked with translating the human experience for the rest of us?

You can write new worlds into being.

You can start a revolution.

You can remake the world into a more thoughtful place.

Who better than you to channel power?

No one.

4

LEARN AND DISCERN

WE'VE GONE OVER the process, activations, and an overview of some tools for making magic, but we've yet to talk about the most important part: How do you know if you're on the right track?

With so many tools to choose from, and even more we've yet to explore, it can be really difficult to figure out if it's working for you. The voice in your head that you may think is your intuition could actually be anxiety, telling you to steer clear of this tool or technique to keep you safe (and small). And let's not forget that creativity is cyclical, not linear, so you may be in a very natural fallow period where *no* tool or technique is working. And it isn't supposed to! That doesn't mean there's anything wrong with the cards or stars or *you*; in fact, there's something very right with you if you're in the middle of the reset your mind, body, and spirit need.

This is where it's important to learn and discern as you go through the rest of the book, and then take your practice beyond it. Remember: Magic is about working in the sacred space between order and chaos, for that's where your true power lies. First, we adhere to the order part of that equation by learning the "rules" for working with these tools. Then, we'll throw in a dash of chaos by allowing your own inner voice to guide you toward which tools to use and how to use them in your own unique way.

It's important to note that the results of this will be different for everyone based on our personal preferences, past experiences, and cosmic blueprint. Some of us may need to stick closer to the "order" side, so we may become wholehearted devotees to reading tarot with traditional meanings and using tried-and-true spreads. Others may feel more magical and powerful when they shift closer to the "chaos" side and create their own spreads, meanings, and even their own decks.

But first, we should all aim to start with a curious, open mind as we learn about time-honored traditions that ancient mystics have held in high regard for thousands of years. As you read through the following sections on astrology, nature magic, tarot, and more, give yourself the time and space to sit with the information, especially if it's brand-new to you. Try to peel away the layers of doubt (for now), and erase everything you've heard about these practices in the past so it's just you and the information on the page, in this present moment. If something doesn't make sense or seems weird, try not to instantly reject it as untrue. Sit with it. Ask questions of yourself. Some starter questions to consider are:

✦ *Why does this information make me uncomfortable?*
✦ *What have I learned about [blank] that conflicts with what I'm learning now?*

+ *Did I come into this new knowledge with preconceived notions?*
+ *What notions do I have about the kind of people who believe this stuff?*

That last question, in particular, is pretty powerful. Many times, we dig our heels in on learning new information or upending our current viewpoint because we're worried about what other people will think, and with good reason. Society hasn't been kind to creatives . . . pretty much ever. There are so many archetypes of the "unstable creative" burned into the collective already, and add to that the idea that we're also reading the stars to inform our process? Whoo boy. As if we didn't already have enough to deal with when it comes to trying to explain our art, but *also* trying to explain our magic? It's a lot.

Still, we can't let the perceptions of others dictate what's best for us and our work. Our first allegiance is always to our true self, and by extension, the parts of ourselves that we express out into the world through our projects. Other people matter (they're the consumers of our art, after all) but only *after* we've worked through the intricacies of our own beliefs, process, and magic. They consume the finished product. Frankly, they don't even really need to know how we got there.

After you've given yourself some time and space to absorb new information, you want to take a minute to discern what it all means for you, personally. The definition of *discern* is to distinguish one thing from another, but in this sense, we're talking about your ability to *recognize the flicker of your own magic* through your intuition. It can happen while you're reading about something new, or it can show up when you're online shopping for tarot cards, or when you try out a tool for the first or four hundredth time. It can and will happen anytime, really. You just have to notice when it does.

A lot of creatives I work with have mentioned that they have a hard time differentiating between the flicker of their own magic and anxiety. It's a fair worry, and one that I've run into in the past, too. At the time it's happening, anxiety can *feel* a lot like intuition. But there's one key difference between the two, and as long as you have that information in the back of your mind, you'll always be able to tell the difference.

Anxiety plays on your past wounds. It disempowers you.

Intuition gives you information about your possible future. It helps you to see things from a different perspective so you can make empowered choices.

Whenever you're learning something new or exploring a new tool and you get a twinge in your gut, a sense of knowing, or some other form of intuitive hit, sit with it for a moment. Pause. Breathe. Then ask yourself if what you're feeling can be related to something or someone that's hurt you in the past. Maybe you've learned, through life experience, that following your intuition causes pain. Or that honoring your creativity and saying no to others has led to hurt feelings in the past.

First, that is extremely real, and there's no judgment here for feeling that way. If it comes up for you, just acknowledge that it's your heart's way of trying to keep you safe and that you understand what it's trying to do here, but for now, Anxiety's gotta stay home with a snack and nap while you and Intuition ride off into the sunset.

Once you've acknowledged it, anxiety tends to get quieter so your intuition can speak up. But here's the tricky part: Intuition can sound absolutely bonkers sometimes, while anxiety seems to make sense, at least in the moment. Honestly, why wouldn't it? Anxiety is speaking to you from your past. It has witnessed everything that's happened to you in your life and is giving you advice based on experience. It's the "order" here, and we tend to believe that logic and order are what keep the world chugging along.

Maybe they do, on a day-to-day level. Logic and order keep us on schedule. They keep us from blowing up our lives to buy a one-way plane ticket to Belize on a random Monday afternoon. They also keep us from any sort of chaos, good or bad, intentional or unintentional. They keep us from the secret ingredient to magic.

The hardest part is trusting yourself enough to entertain your intuition's off-the-wall ideas. We know that we need a bit of chaos to really tap into our magic, our source of power, and that means sometimes taking a detour on our chosen path. There have been many times I had a carefully crafted outline for a story, and my intuition decided to take me off-roading halfway through the story. It's a little bit terrifying, to be honest, but in my experience, the story has always been better for it (and required less editing) in the end.

In the following sections, we'll go over the tools, activations, and process in greater detail so that you'll be able to close this book with a much deeper understanding of which tools resonate with you, how to hear your intuition clearer, and, of course, to tap into your highest creative potential. We'll start with the tools first, giving you a chance to learn and discern what you think about them, and if they have a place in your creativity toolbox going forward. Then we'll go over the process of accessing your magic at the highest degree, with examples of how you can tap into certain tools and activations for each part of the process. Ultimately, you'll end up with a guide to choosing your tools and how they can work for different aspects of your creative life.

You get to decide how and what you do with this information. You get to piece it together in a way that makes sense for *you,* your goals, and your magic. Which, in my opinion, is the ultimate act of creative expression.

Now let's get to it.

· ·

SPELLWORK: YOUR MAGIC DICTIONARY

Go back to the page in your notebook where you wrote down the words *magic, creativity, creative, activation,* and *tool.* After reading through part 1, you should have enough information to scribble down an explanation for each concept. To break it down in simple terms, you can also jot down the following:

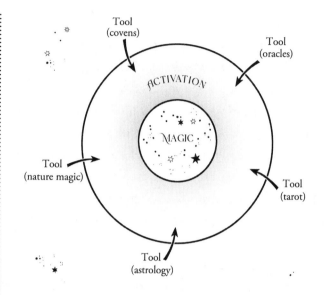

Magic: *a conversation between the universe and your heart*
Creativity: *what you do with the wisdom gleaned from that conversation*
Creative: *someone who makes something*
Activation: *a state of being that allows us to listen to our magic with greater ease*
Tool: *a concrete device or method that gets us to an activation*

Now over to you. Reread through these definitions and decide if they resonate with you. If not, feel free to write your own version or even add on to the ones

I've created. The point is for you to have a strong understanding of magic from which to build your creative foundation on going forward. When you feel like you have that covered, you're ready to keep journeying onward.

• •

SPELLWORK: YOUR CREATIVITY TOOLBOX

In this exercise, we'll start to put together a creativity toolbox that you can continue to add to even after you're finished with this book. Turn to a fresh page in your notebook. Label the top of the page "My Creativity Toolbox." Then divide the page into three separate columns. Label the first column "Tool," the second column "Works For," and the third "Rating." In the rating column, draw ten small circles, stars, hearts, or whatever symbol you'd like. You'll color them in later.

As you learn about a tool, write it down in the first column. Then, write down the part of your creative process for which you think this tool might be helpful, based on what you discover in this book. If you aren't sure and would rather experiment with a tool before filling in this column, feel free to leave it blank. Finally, once you spend time getting to

know a tool, rate its efficacy. Some questions to ask
yourself as you rate your tools are:

+ *Is it easy to use, or can I see how it will be-
  come easier for me to use in time?*
+ *Do I enjoy using it?*
+ *Does it feel empowering?*
+ *Does it get me closer to my magic and cre-
  ative potential?*

You'll rate each tool on a scale from one to ten
by coloring in your symbols. Remember: You're
allowed to change and grow, and the tools you
use will inevitably change, too. This is an exercise
in gaining clarity so you can tap into your magic
with greater ease. If at any point this becomes la-
borious and feels purposeless, you can always dis-
continue it.

CREATIVITY TOOLBOX

TOOL NAME	WORKS FOR	RATING
Ex. tarot	Clarifying ideas, character, development, etc.	●●●●●●○○○

....

PART II

THE TOOLS

5

Nature Magic 101

If I had to pick the worst month of the year, it'd be February. It's the last full month of winter, the snow-lined streets in Michigan have started to look more crusty than cottony, and I always, inevitably, end up sick in bed with a killer cold.

While February and I aren't on speaking terms, learning to align with nature's rhythms has helped heal my relationship with this time of year. Nature wisdom teaches us that there's a season for everything, and February's rhythm (in the Northern Hemisphere, at least) calls us to rest and recharge before spring arrives. For someone who prefers to move at a breakneck speed, this is a big ask. It's also why February has consistently taken me down for the count. When I choose to sync up and roll with winter's rhythms, I tend to have an easier time of it. I get sick less. I get more done. We're all happier for it.

With listening comes healing, and with healing comes a new perspective, a new vision, and the internal resources to not only get through a month, season, or year but to thrive in it.

HUMANS · NATURE: THE DREAM TEAM

Just like I have my personal issue with February, humans, as a whole, have their own baggage with nature. Most of this has to do with Western society's conception of what nature *is*. There are various arguments for when humans started to see themselves as separate from nature. Some say it started with the Christian teaching of man's "dominion over nature," and others say it has to do with the relentless and exploitive expansion of the West, but either way, that's a discussion for a different book.

For the purposes of this book, what matters is that the connection between nature and humans was broken somewhere in history, and that's only been to our detriment. Without a strong connection to the cycles and rhythms of our planet, companies, brands, and influential people can convince us to follow "their way" for greater fulfillment and productivity, even when they don't have our best interest at heart. But when you connect with nature, you're connecting with the deepest parts of yourself—and *you* will always have your best interest at heart.

Let's be real: Humans are mammals. And like other mammals, we rely on the Earth to feed and care for us. By tapping into our planet's natural cycles, the Earth can breathe a sigh of relief. We're finally listening, and it can fully provide us with the wisdom we need to unlock our greatest creative potential.

CIRCLES AND CYCLES

Whether it's the indigenous medicine wheel or the wheel of the year in paganism, the circle represents an endless cycle. For every ending, there's another beginning, and when you think you've finished one adventure, the circle shows us that another journey is starting.

Both the medicine wheel and the wheel of the year are divided into four pieces, a pair of lines intersecting in the center to create four sections, or pieces. In the medicine wheel, each section represents a direction, and the wheel of the year is divided into the four seasons. A compass rose is also a circle divided into four sections representing north, south, east, and west.

The elliptical path of celestial bodies loops back on itself, bringing with it the ending of one cosmic cycle and the beginning of another. The zodiacal wheel is a circle separated into twelve houses and four seasons. The lunar cycle is also a circle with four primary phases (new moon, first quarter moon, full moon, and last quarter moon). The life cycles of frogs and butterflies and the water cycle are all represented by a circle with at least four critical "turning points." And get this: If you're someone who ovulates, you also have a cycle with four critical turning points—the follicular phase, ovulation, the luteal phase, and menstruation.

Humans are wired to sync up with a circular rhythm, these completely natural ebbs and flows. Unfortunately, Western society reveres a more linear time line that values productivity over all else. But human innovation and creativity don't adhere to tight deadlines and societal pressure. Creativity, just like the sun, the moon, times, tides, and the seasons, has its own circle and cycle.

THE CREATIVITY CYCLE

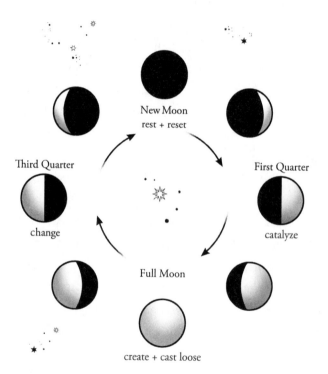

Like the moon, creativity isn't meant to reflect light into the world at all times. The creativity cycle is the natural ebb and flow of internal work and external production, and when we can figure out where we currently are in the cycle and go with it, instead of fighting against it, we can create with less friction and a lot more magic.

THE NEW MOON PHASE

Also known as the *winter* and *water* phase, the new moon phase of the cycle is what some creatives might consider a fallow period. In winter, seeds are working beneath the snow and soil to prepare for a busy spring. Plants are resting so that when the snow thaws, they're ready to grow again. In astrology, Neptune and the moon represent the water element. Neptune is the planet of the subconscious, and the moon represents self-nurturing. Just like a chart is incomplete without those two celestial bodies, the creativity cycle is incomplete without this critical period of rest.

To the outside world, it doesn't look like there's much creative work going on when you're in the new moon phase. It may look like a lot of Netflix and aimless wandering, but *this part is just as important to the cycle as any other phase.* Flowers can't skip through winter even if they'd rather bloom, and neither can you. The harder you try to push against this fallow period, the more difficult it is to finally get out of it. The key word for this phase is *surrender.*

As you move through the new moon phase, you'll eventually come to a point where you start to get the urge to create again. It may be just a nudge at first. Instead of taking a nap, you might feel like opening a new doc on your laptop. Just to play. Or you may have a dream about a new idea and you find you're actually excited about it instead of exhausted by the thought of starting over again. When you've gotten here, you're officially shifting into the waxing crescent phase, well on your way to the next turning point, the first quarter phase.

THE FIRST QUARTER PHASE

The first quarter phase is also known as the *spring* and *earth* phase of the cycle. Like spring, this is a time of increasing productivity that's visible to the outside world, and steadfast earth energy can help us get started. During this phase, exactly half of the moon's surface is visible in the night sky, while the other half remains dark. It's important to remember this as we jump into a new painting or manuscript; there's still internal work to be done.

This first quarter phase is a mix of putting pen to paper and making things happen, while also planning, resting, and thinking. In early spring, the ground is still barren and untenable. We need to till the soil and plant before we see things starting to grow. This is a time of opening that fresh doc, giving yourself a deadline, creating a plan, getting to the art store, and stocking up on the supplies you need. It's both preparation *and* productivity, while simultaneously learning what this new project will require of you. The key word of this phase is *begin*.

As you communicate with this new project and find your bearings, you'll begin to pick up speed. The words start to come a little easier, you can tap into a flow state, and you start to become more outwardly productive. You've made it to the waxing gibbous phase, which comes right before the full moon.

The Full Moon Phase

Next comes the full moon phase, also known as the *summer* and *fire* phase. Here the moon is at its brightest—its entire surface is lit up in full reflection of the sun's light. This is a time of major productivity *and* pleasure. By summertime, the hard work of spring is mostly finished, and now it's time to take a step back to allow your project to bloom.

It's a time of greater ease, where you can rely on other resources to help you succeed. Just like plants can't grow without the sun and soil, and the moon can't glow without a relationship with the sun, we, too, look to our friends and chosen family to help us out in this phase. If you're mid-project, you may want to run some ideas by a friend. Or if you've been working hard, you may feel the urge to take a socialization break for a few hours or even a few days.

This phase is all about looking around you at the bountiful resources you already have to help you on the journey, and that includes the people around you. While this may come naturally for some creatives, others may have a tougher time letting others into their process and projects, especially when so much of this work has been solitary up until this point. That's why the key words for this phase are *let go*.

As you move through this full moon phase, the moon begins to wane. You may feel a call to go back to a project with a new perspective, especially if you've taken a break from it. Now in the waning gibbous phase, your internal compass calls you back to your work to consider what else it may need.

THE LAST QUARTER PHASE

Finally, we end up on the other side of the moon's ellipse with the last quarter moon. This phase is also considered the *autumn* and *air* phase. Once again, our moon is half-hidden, half-illuminated, and it calls us to wrap up our work. Autumn is the season of endings; trees shed their leaves; plants trade their blooms for berries so pollinators can carry off their seeds before the ground freezes over. Animals leave the North for warmer climates or fall into a winter slumber. The ones that stay store food to make it through fallow times.

In the creativity cycle, this is a pivot from buoyant, fully expressed creativity to taking care of all the loose ends that need to be tied up before you can rest. For writers, this often looks like revisions and editing, or finally turning in a book. For artists, it could look like placing that final clear coat on your work, and for musicians, it could be applying the lyrics to the beat. This phase requires that we take care of the remaining details, which is why its key words are *wrap up*.

As the moon continues to wane, you start powering down after several seasons of sweat, tears, and love. Finally, you end the cycle at the dark moon phase, the one to three days before the new moon where the moon is completely dark.

HOW TO SYNC WITH THE CYCLES

Syncing up with this little slice of nature magic is easier than it may seem. It's the first step that's the hardest: being honest with yourself about where you are in the cycle.

You may desperately *want* to be basking in a full moon/ summer phase, where you're ready to relax with your creative friends and source your inspiration from different people, media, and adventures. But if you aren't real with yourself about where you actually are, you can't sync up and leverage the creativity cycle for your advantage. If you're in a fallow period, a new moon phase, then you're in a new moon phase. *And there is nothing wrong with that.* All parts of the cycle are of equal importance and are relative to the process.

You may be wondering if your personal creativity cycle should line up with the actual season or moon phase going on outside your window. For example: Should you be in a summer season while the days are long and hot? A new moon phase in sync with the moonless sky above your head? The answer is a resounding nope. Sure, there are gifts to syncing up with what's going on inside to what's happening outside. If you're in a productive spring phase creatively, you'll most likely get an extra boost of energy from the lengthening days and new buds happening concurrently, which in turn fuels your drive and motivation. But nature always provides us with gifts, no matter which season we're experiencing. If, creatively, you're in a contemplative autumn, or last quarter moon, but outside it's summer, you can still leverage the vibrancy that summer has to offer in your creative practice. Maybe instead of outwardly producing, you'll channel some of that summer magic into reflecting on your process, cleaning up your work space, and getting ready to sink into the deep rest of your upcoming personal winter. The point is: There's always something to learn and leverage from both personal and external cycles.

Once you've identified where you are, all you really have to do is hang tight and let the cycle work through *you* as you work through the cycle. Just like you can't skip a season in the year, you also can't skip a phase. If you did absolutely nothing, you would eventually move through the cycle on your own, but there are also tools you can use to help you shift through with greater ease and alignment.

SPELLWORK: TRACK YOUR PHASE

After spending some time with the creativity cycle and the descriptions of its phases, which phase do you think you're in right now? Remember, you can always be in an "in-between phase," like a waxing crescent phase, moving toward a first quarter moon, but not quite there yet.

Once you think you've got it down, go back to the creativity toolbox you started in your notebook. At the top of the page, write down which phase you're in now. You could even draw a small symbol or doodle to represent that phase, like a mini moon or something else that's meaningful to you. Then write a single word beside it that describes your creativity *right now*.

The magic appears when you fully own and accept what's happening within you at this very moment. So be honest with yourself. What is one word to describe your creativity at the moment? Maybe it's *prolific* or *powerful* or *personal*. But if it's something more like *fallow* or *far away*, that is completely okay. The point is to consciously recognize and put words to how this particular phase in the creativity cycle feels to you. That way, you'll be able to recognize where you are right away, and you'll have a toolbox ready and waiting for you to help you through it.

For the rest of this book, we're going to focus on filling out your creativity toolbox for *only this phase* that you've identified. You'll learn how to use the tools and work the process through any phase, but first it's important to help you along in the phase you're already in. That way, you can test these tools and strategies against your experience, in real time, to see what works.

NATURE MAGIC TOOLS

Here you'll find a few of my favorite starter tools for tapping into nature's magic, medicine, and seasons. It's important to note that *nature magic* is a broad term that also encompasses practices involving the elements, astrology (planets are part of nature, too), and even tarot. Nature is in every one of the sacred arts, because it touches everything we do. For the purpose of this book, the nature magic tools I'm including here are earth-based tools that focus on nature as we experience it just outside our door. Their purpose is to help us gain a sense of steadiness no matter what cycle, season, or phase we're in.

Tree Talk

Spend time observing nature and deciphering what it's trying to say. Even if you're in a full blossom full moon phase in the dead of winter where you're located, we can't deny that the seasons affect us. A lot of creatives I know tend to do their profoundest work while the rest of the world goes underground in winter. It's quieter, there's less distraction, and there's room to think.

Consider what trees, in particular, are up to during the same phase or season you're in for hints on how to move forward. For example, if you're in a last quarter moon, or autumn phase, think about what autumn traditionally represents. It's the last hurrah as deciduous trees shed what no longer nourishes them. Just as the moon allows in the darkness, the trees also let go of their leaves without resistance.

Look at the parts of your life that have loose ends to tie up, whether they're directly related to your art or not. Let go of old clothes that no longer fit, toss old journals, reorganize your to-do list. Make like autumn and let it all go.

Set Seasonal Goals

We tend to think in small chunks—daily to-do lists and weekly goals. The planners on the shelves in big-box stores usually include a monthly overview, but what about seasons? In nature, time is measured in change, however slight, in the natural environment outside your window. Even while you're in the midst of a blistering summer, the wisdom of the flora and fauna around you has already started to prepare for autumn's arrival.

In your notebook or grimoire, create separate pages for spring, summer, autumn, and winter. On each page, reflect on what each season means for you personally. Maybe you're rejuvenated by the heat of summer and it's when you feel most creative. Or perhaps you love the fresh burst of life that comes with spring's arrival and you find your best ideas tend to crop up then. You can jot down memories, your favorite parts of each season, or even the parts you don't love. All this information can help you set reasonable and attainable seasonal goals.

Once you've filled your pages, take a closer look at the information you've gathered, then create a goal for each season. For example, I know I tend to be on the go a lot in the summer, so I keep my summer goals pretty light and breezy so I can enjoy the season, then go heavier in the fall. Find your own patterns and preferences, then go from there.

Environmental Research

Explore the natural flora and fauna in your area. If you're outdoorsy, take yourself on a hike and observe what's out there in real time. If you'd rather hang out indoors, the internet is your friend. Collect a list of plants, trees, flowers, insects, reptiles, mammals, and birds in your notebook. You could even jot down a few ideas, thoughts, or memories that you associate with each one. Let's go back to the story of my nature bestie, the Japanese maple from chapter 1, as an example of this work. Ironically (or maybe not), I also have a Japanese maple tree in the front yard of my current house. In my grimoire, I created a section just for this tree where I've dried and pressed its leaves and have journaled around them about feeling magic, the blissful and not-so-blissful childhood memories I associate with this tree, and so on.

The purpose of this is twofold. On the practical side, I now know a lot more about this tree, including its scent, its textures, and what the whisper-thin veins in its purplish leaves feel like, which only deepens my writing and drawing practices. On the esoteric side, I've churned up all kinds of emotional fodder that I can and do use when I'm creating, either by inserting tiny slivers of memories into my projects or by tapping into the feelings that this tree brings forth when I want to channel those emotions into my art. And on the personal development front, environmental research such as this also helps me to see what wounds still need tending and may even give me clues as to how to do so.

* * *

Think of this work as a nature magic index that you're curating. As you learn more about making magic, this list will be exceptionally helpful. You may even find that you build a relationship with some of these wild things, and they become sacred partners in your process.

6

THE ELEMENTS

MAGIC AND THE classical elements have an exceptionally deep relationship. In fact, it's pretty difficult to learn about astrology, tarot, nature magic, or any number of sacred tools without *also* learning about the elements. You can do this concurrently, of course. I learned the basics behind the elements while also learning tarot, and then I learned even *more* while studying astrology. That said, if you go into learning these tools with some background on the elements and their relationship to magic, it makes it a whole lot easier to remember card meanings and planetary patterns. Plus, the elements themselves are their own potent tool that you can leverage when listening to your magic.

From alchemists to astrologers to modern witches, the elements have been referenced as an entrance point to magic throughout history. And it makes sense, if you think about it. We've discussed how magic happens when you find your personal balance between cosmic order and chaos, and the elements are just an extension of that theory. Think of adding in the elements as a way to target the specific kind of magic you need for any given situation. Maybe you need a little bit of the earth element to help you feel grounded and stable, but you'll also add in a touch of water to help you remain open-hearted as you craft your project. Maybe you need some of the air element to help you think logically about a problem, along with a dash of fire so you'll actually take action. The elements are a nature-based tool that can be used on their own, yet they also form a firm foundation for all the other tools you'll learn about in this book. Let's take a deep dive into each one, its mystical meaning, and where it tends to show up in some other tools and techniques.

WATER: THE ANCIENT LIFE-GIVER

Civilizations throughout history have placed special emphasis on water as the ultimate giver of life. Whether we're talking about the "primordial soup" we all came from or the element that makes up 60 percent of the human body, water is both what makes us and keeps us alive.

In religious traditions, water often plays a symbolic role in rituals and rites of passage. In Christianity, a baptism marks the beginning of one's relationship with God. Water that's been blessed is consumed after puja in Hinduism. Ritual washing is also a part of many other religions, including Judaism, Islam, Buddhism, and more. Water and its life-giving essence have acted as a vehicle between humans and the divine for thousands of years.

In mystical terms, water represents the flow of our subconscious, including all the emotions that we tend to suppress beneath the surface. Water is also a symbol of healing and purification, as evidenced by how our bodies help us move stagnant emotions so we can process them. Isak Dinesen once said, "The cure for anything is salt water: sweat, tears, or the sea." There's a deep truth to that. It's through water that our bodies can release and move into a period of restoration.

If you already know a bit about the elements, you may have read that water also represents meditation, music, significant relationships, and rest and rejuvenation. In fact, *I've* also said all those things when I've taught about astrology or tarot. All those associations are true, but at its core, water symbolizes the *consciousness of our emotions.*

And when do our emotions tend to come out to play with (or punch) us? When we find ourselves in a relationship or listening to music that pulls at our heartstrings, or when we allow our bodies and minds to actually rest. But going a little deeper than just feeling our feelings, the water element shows us how to access the wisdom our emotions have for us.

This is simpler for some than others. If you're someone who is naturally very feely and in tune with your emotions, you may already be pretty adept when it comes to interpreting the universal messages they have for you. But if you don't really relate to big feelings, figuring out the language of water and emotions can be more difficult. The truth is, we all have an affinity toward one or two elements and tend to be able to interpret them better than the others, and the water element may not be your strong suit. Yet the more you learn the language of each element, the more information you can glean about yourself, your creativity, your projects, and how you make magic in the world. You don't have to be fluent in all elemental languages, but it helps to at least be proficient.

Imagine how much easier it would be to sit down in front of your project and feel something other than sheer and utter terror. What if you could honor your emotions—*all* of them—without fear instead of forcing them back down, where they'll inevitably fester until given the opportunity to bubble up again? What if you could recognize your feelings as sacred messengers, whispering to you what to heal, what to restore, what to let go of, so you can fully access your magic and power, instead of viewing them as inconveniences to be tamed? And, most important, what if you could learn to channel the wisdom of your emotions into a potent force within your work, subsequently touching the lives of many?

That's the promise of the water element, but only when we learn to honor, accept, and work in symbiosis with it. That means getting comfortable with our own depths, including the murkier parts we may not want to see.

When we start to delve into some of the mystical associations of water, it helps to look at its physical attributes first. Water is fluid, boundaryless, and, when it's at its best, clear and refreshing. It can shock you if you aren't expecting that ocean wave or warm-weather downpour, or it can come in trickles of relief. It softens sunbaked soil and parched lips and makes our systems run efficiently from the inside out. So, too, does it help us to listen to the emotional essence of our creativity. We'll dive into a myriad of ways to work with water energy in the following sections, but some simple options include taking

a bath, swimming, listening to music, and anything that unlocks your emotions.

THE MAGIC OF WATER

As discussed in the previous section, water shows up in some
form in just about every tool you can use to access magic.
From astrology to tarot to nature magic, water reminds us
that there's wisdom to be mined from our emotions (yes,
even the hard ones).

Let's start with the cosmos. In astrology, water shows up
to describe a trio of zodiac signs: Cancer, Scorpio, and Pisces. All three are different and have different desires, wants,
and needs (more on that in the astrology chapter), but each
of them places an important emphasis on emotions. These
signs are particularly sensitive—to other people, their environment, and the unseen—and their intuition tends to come
to them in the form of feelings. In terms of creativity, water
signs tend to use their feelings as fuel to create works of art.
Along with the signs, some of the celestial bodies pertinent
to modern astrology are also considered "watery" in nature.
Our moon is often associated with the water element, as it
represents our inner life (not to mention it also causes our
ocean tides to ebb and flow). Neptune, the blue planet of
dreams and imagination, is also associated with water, and in
classical astrology, so is Venus, which rules love of all kinds.

Bringing it back down to Earth, water also shows up in
the cards. In the classic Rider-Waite tarot deck, water is represented by one of the four suits in the Minor Arcana, the
suit of cups. Like a chalice waiting to be filled, the cups

represent connections, emotions, and the relationships that "fill our cup" with all kinds of feelings.

And, of course, we know that water plays an integral role in nature. Not only is it an essential, life-giving force for all the plants, trees, and wildlife, but it acts as a conduit for rest, healing, and peace. Its symbology shows up in movies and music that includes a bubbling brook or a thunderstorm to help calm our minds and bodies. In seasonal magic, water is aligned with the winter season, which is quiet and reflective. Winter's arrival hushes the noise from the external world so we can give our intuitive nudges and emotions the time and space they need to deliver their wisdom.

SPELLWORK: FIND YOUR WATER POWER OBJECT

Whether you identify strongly with the water element or you'd rather keep all your emotions tucked way, way down there (trust me, I get it), there's still so much value in connecting with this element. Like I mentioned, everything in creation has been made through some combination of the four elements, whether it's an entire bucket of water to create clay, or the water vapor in the air to create a touch of humidity. For you to access your full creative potential and every last drop of your magic, you'll have to become acquainted with water, too.

For this exercise, you'll start to think about how you want to cultivate your relationship with the water element, then later, you'll find or purchase an object that represents it. First, open up your notebook to a fresh page and write "Water" at the top. Then spend some time doodling objects, people, places, and memories that remind you of water. These can be things associated physically with water, like a memory of a family vacation by the sea, or metaphysically, like a relationship in your life that feels healing and peaceful. Nothing you draw is wrong here. Just be open and let yourself explore.

When you feel like you have a solid number of drawings, look back at the page. Is there an object that shows up in more than one doodle, or is there something that could represent more than one doodle? For example, if you drew an image of the ocean, a relationship, and rain, is there an emotion that connects all those things together for you? Maybe you have fond memories of the ocean and you love the sound of summer rain, so you could choose a simple heart-shaped object. Other excellent options include small objects that you have a personal history with, trinkets from ancestors or relatives, seashells or other objects that come from the ocean, blue crystals, moon-related objects, or anything that reminds you of peace and rest.

Once you've decided on your object, write it down on your "Water" page. You don't have to go searching for it now—that work comes later. For this moment, you're only identifying your object while you're soaking in this new understanding of the water element.

Circle your object on the page. If you'd like, you can also surround it with a few words or phrases that represent how you hope your relationship with this element will grow. As you become more attuned to water, you open up a new avenue through which to create with your magic—through your emotions—and the more avenues you cultivate, the more powerful you feel and your creations become. It's not always easy to work in the watery emotional realm, but it's always worth it.

When you're finished, close your notebook and get ready to step into the next element.

EARTH: THE SACRED STABILIZER

While water moves freely, its complementary element, earth, provides a container for it to flow. Where water is fluid and boundaryless, earth is stable and dense. It, too, is a giver of life, like water, but it does so by providing a safe, nourishing container in which something can grow. It's the unsung hero of the elements, the one that doesn't necessarily get a lot of attention but is absolutely necessary for getting things done.

The human body may be mostly made of water, but it's our bones that hold us upright. They add structure and form to the body so that we can go about our day-to-day lives, and move our skin sacks from our couches to our computers so we can make art. Similarly, the earth element provides us with stability, structure, and a vehicle through which to make our dreams a concrete reality. Earth symbolizes *the consciousness of the physical body.*

As much as we sometimes don't want to admit it, we're physical beings. We have to be. Anyone with chronic pain will tell you, you can't ignore your body. And while many creatives prefer to play in the realms of imagination and possibility, it's this body that gets us from point A to point B, that takes us to our desks or easels so we can actually do the work of making what we want to make.

Ancient mystics and religious leaders understood this primal need to feel connected to our bodies, our people, and our beliefs in a tangible way. This is one reason why we've built sacred temples and secluded graveyards—so we have a tactile, physical space that we can visit whenever we're ready to process our emotions, intuition, and pain. I also suspect it's why so many important milestones in life are signified with food—feasts, potlucks, and birthday cakes. The experience of engaging your five physical senses while emotions are running high helps us to anchor what we're feeling.

The earth element can also provide us with a sense of safety so any subconscious emotions can finally bubble to the surface to be processed. There's a reason why the practice of yoga has withstood the test of time and why therapy that includes physical senses, like eye movement desensitization and reprocessing (EMDR), can be extremely powerful in helping to shift stuck emotions. Earth reminds us that physical spaces, including the one we interact with every second of every day—our bodies—need the same tenderness and attention that we give to our dreams, relationships, and ambitions.

When we think about earth and what it represents, it helps to consider its attributes. Earth is stable, for sure, but can sometimes be rigid and unyielding. There's earth that is fertile soil, ready to provide the perfect amount of support and nutrients to help a seedling flourish, and there's earth that is dry, rigid, and untenable. While earth provides a solid container in which to make things happen, it also requires input from the other elements—water, air, and fire—to make it fertile, depending on what you need for a certain project. It can be loose and compliant, like sand slipping through your fingers, for a project that requires less constraints. It can be as solid as a boulder, if you need it to be, to set impenetrable boundaries. The most important thing is that you know exactly how to work with the earth element to create a sense of stability, structure, and safety. Some options for getting to know the earth element include strength-training exercise, nature walks, and any practice that brings you back into your physical body.

THE MAGIC OF EARTH

Just like water, the earth element also shows up in many sacred tools. In astrology, there is a trio of zodiac signs that embody earth: Taurus, Virgo, and Capricorn. All three have their distinctions, and what motivates and inspires them may be different, but they have plenty of similarities, too. Each of these signs prefers order to chaos, stability to surprises. At their core, these archetypes understand how to tap into and leverage the unique gifts of the earth element more than any of the other signs. Venus can be considered an "earthy" planet, as well as a "watery" one, in that it invites us to indulge in our physical senses in pursuit of love, beauty, and art. On the other end of the spectrum is Saturn, which represents order and structure, just like the earth element.

Earth energy also shows up in the cards. In most tarot decks, earth is represented by the suit of pentacles (also sometimes called *coins*). This suit illuminates what we need to know about physical resources that we need to survive—like our homes, careers, and finances. From the Ace of Pentacles to the Ten of Pentacles, the journey through these cards shows us the grit and determination it takes to harbor the resources you need throughout your life.

We also know that the foundation of all life is earth. Nature shows us that a nutrient-dense foundation gives us a strong, healthy starting point from which we can grow into ourselves as we plumb our inner depths. At the same time, earth also shows us that life can bloom in any kind of circumstance—from cacti in the sunbaked desert to mushrooms in waterlogged decay—as long as we allow ourselves to be surprised and delighted by what grows in the foundation we've established. There's no room for judgment when it comes to working with earth; there's only the steadfast toiling, and the alchemic mixing of air, fire, and water within it, to create the exact base layer we want and need for our projects. This is why earth is associated with building a strong foundation in the spring season.

. . . .

SPELLWORK: FIND YOUR EARTH POWER OBJECT

Just as you did for the water element, you'll create a fresh space in your magical notebook to explore your earth power object. Start by writing the word *Earth* at the top of the page. Then let your mind wander. Think about the times you've been particularly connected to the earth, whether it was during a rigorous hike in the mountains or while listening to pebbles crunch beneath your sneakers on an early-morning walk.

Spend some time doodling and jotting down notes about the earth element—memories, sensations, your relationship to your physical body, routines, structures, and your home. Once you feel like you've extracted enough information, do the same as you did for the water element. Consider if any of these thoughts, ideas, and drawings represent the type of relationship you'd like to cultivate with the earth element or ways in which you already naturally connect with it. If you're having trouble thinking of something, remember: There's no wrong answer. Go with your gut.

When in doubt, you can choose any objects that remind you of earth—plant seeds, stones, or dark-colored, opaque crystals. Small pieces of wood and bark also work wonderfully, as well as pressed plants or flowers or other items you may have collected while out in nature. When you've decided on your object, write it down on your "Earth" page, along with a few words or phrases to describe your budding relationship with this element.

∫IR: THE MERCURIAL MESSENGER

Imagine you're taking a walk through your neighborhood. As you turn the street corner, you catch a whiff of something. Maybe it's spring lilac in full bloom or the tang of barbecue from your neighbor's back porch. Maybe it's a mix of pungent sewer water and powdered sugar from the bakery on the corner, but even if it's unpleasant, the scent still coaxes a memory from the back of your mind. Maybe you walked these same streets with your grandpa or you grabbed a croissant from the bakery just yesterday. As you continue on your walk, the sounds of rushing cars and dogs barking flood your ears. You can even feel the electricity of an impending storm in the breeze, and you can thank the air element for all of it.

Like water, air is fluid, flexible, and brings important information to our attention. But while water helps our deepest desires and emotions bubble into consciousness, air delivers a plethora of information from all four corners of the Earth. The air element is the great dot-connector, the invisible messenger that brings to light new information in its many forms so that we can form our own logical conclusions. Air is the *consciousness of our thoughts*.

When we understand how to work with the air element, we learn to work in collaboration with our thoughts instead of pushing in the opposite direction of the wind. Instead of allowing our thoughts to whip into a whirlwind, taking us through an internal, often illogical spiral, we can quell a storm from forming in the first place. We can learn the language of our thoughts and the message they want to deliver, and then make our best attempt to let them go on their way, just as the breeze does.

I get that it isn't as easy as it sounds. As someone whose best friend calls her a "chaos being," I fully understand that letting go of irrational thoughts is, well, sometimes impossible. What I do know is that my creativity is so much more fluid and flexible when my thoughts aren't disruptive and that it's easier to move from one aspect of a project to the next without friction.

There's a reason why the phrase *clearing the air* has been around since the 1400s. It literally refers to the way the wind blows away the clouds after a storm. Metaphorically, we use the phrase to describe the lingering sense of unease that hangs in the air after an argument. And let's not forget the ritual of burning incense and sacred herbs in just about every religious tradition throughout history, often as a method of purification. Intuitively, we've always understood that even though the air around us is invisible, it can and does hold a ton of information and insight that we can use to our advantage—once we know how to harness it. To get to know the air element on a basic level, consider practices like burning incense, deep breathing exercises, and any practice that engages your mind and nervous system.

THE MAGIC OF AIR

When it comes to sacred tools, the air element reminds us that there's a place for logic and intellect in making magic, too. The zodiac signs of Gemini, Libra, and Aquarius are all associated with air, and each one has their own special way of tapping into the strengths (and let's be honest, weaknesses) of this element. All three signs in the air trio are intellectual, quick-witted, and endlessly curious. All three also love to connect seemingly dissimilar things to create something truly unique. Gemini loves to connect people, Libra likes to connect differing aesthetics, and Aquarius feels most comfortable in the realm of ideas, but in truth, all three signs can work with some combination of people, places, and ideas. That's just part of being flexible, fluid air.

Planets in our solar system that embody big air energy are Mercury, Uranus, and Jupiter (although Jupiter has both fiery and watery sides, too). Like its eponym, Mercury the planet is quick-moving and represents communication, travel, and thinking. Uranus is the only planet in our solar system that spins on its side, making it the ruler of innovation, and Jupiter represents teaching, philosophy, and higher education—all very air-heavy activities. Plus, we can't forget that Jupiter is considered a gas giant planet in astronomy.

In the tarot, the air element is represented by the suit of swords. At their best, swords can cut through the extraneous to get to the heart of the matter, often using reasoning and connection to make a case for their argument. Some of the most visceral cards of the tarot are in this suit, including the bleeding heart of the Three of Swords and the utter devastation of the Ten of Swords. These cards may look scary, but when we remember that swords represent the air element and our thoughts, we can consider them from a less intense perspective. They depict thoughts that are hurting us or logic that isn't adding up instead of literal death. And let's be honest, when our thoughts become intrusive, they are extremely painful.

In nature, the wind is what creates a cross-connection between all living things. The breeze carries new seeds from place to place, allowing hybrids of plants and flowers to grow where they've never been before. And pollinators that rely on the air element to carry them, like bees and bats, help to spread seeds, too. In seasonal magic, air is associated with autumn. It's the increased winds that shake loose dead leaves so they can fly free and be reborn into something new come spring. Autumn is also a time where we naturally begin to turn inward. This is the season of contemplation, when we ruminate on where we've been and where we're going. It's where we catch our breath and tidy our minds, relationships, and spaces to get ready for the stillness of winter.

SPELLWORK: FIND YOUR AIR POWER OBJECT

Just as you did in the previous exercises, you'll create a space in your notebook for your "Air" page. Again, you'll spend a moment centering yourself, maybe even imagining a soothing breeze on your skin, and doodle or write any associations you have with the air element. Once you have a good idea of how you'd like to connect with air energy in your creative life, choose an object you'd like to eventually have in your possession to represent your emerging relationship.

If you're stumped, consider choosing one of the following items: feathers (real or fake), smudge sticks, dried herbs for burning, incense cones or sticks, small knickknacks of birds, bees, or other flying animals, and light-colored, translucent crystals. Write down what you will acquire for your object so you don't forget what you chose.

FIRE: THE INSPIRED TRANSFORMER

It's hard to imagine that humans ever lived without electricity, let alone the raw power of fire. The last of the four classical elements that humans engaged with, fire—and learning to work with it—was truly transformative. Not only could we stave off hypothermia and early death, but we could now cook our food to rid it of illness-causing bacteria. Fire power, from a crackling campfire to our blazing sun, warms us, inspires us, and transforms us from the inside out.

A burning fire represents God's presence in Christianity. In Vedic tradition, Agni is the god of fire, tasked with delivering sacrifices to other gods and goddesses, in turn transforming an offering into potent wisdom to be consumed. And we can't forget Prometheus from the Greek tradition, who stole fire from the gods to give it to human beings. Throughout history, fire has been viewed as a quick-burning vehicle from one state of being to another.

That's why this element is associated with anything that quickens the heart—pleasure, passion, joy, play, and inspiration. We all know that a shattered heart and unbearable grief can transform a person, but fire teaches us that there is another way. Joy can be just as potent of a catalyst, as can the kind of passion that you can't shake from head and heart. Fire represents *the consciousness of inspiration.*

It was hard for me to wrap my mind around this for a while. It made sense to me that we absolutely require the emotional bonds of water, stability of earth, and the intellect of air to function as human beings. But inspiration? That seemed a little frivolous. It's not like we *need* inspiration to live and breathe on this planet.

Except, it turns out, we do.

Fire was the last element to come into human awareness, just as we had evolved enough to understand how to use it. Similarly, we are again evolving. This world is more complex than ever, and the only way we're going to be able to solve the climate crisis and end war is through some extremely bad-ass inspiration. We're going to need to be so inspired, so filled with joyous moments on this planet, that we *want* to do something about the problems that plague us. It's this inspiration that we need to be in conversation with to access our willpower—another fire-ruled state of being—to get the job done. Just remember: Fire requires careful tending. It deserves love and attention, lest it burn out of control when we turn our attention from it. If there's anyone in this world that knows what it takes to tend to the fire of inspiration, it's creatives.

What I'm saying is: Trust the inspired artists. We know what to do.

THE MAGIC OF FIRE

The fire trio of zodiac signs shows us how to tap into the passion and pleasure needed to inspire, both themselves and others. Aries, Leo, and Sagittarius each embody passion and raw willpower—for better or worse—and inspire us all to move in the direction of our deepest desires. Aries is the warrior of the zodiac, taking their machetes to the obstacles blocking the path to their goals. Leo reminds us that, like our sun, we can and should shine in our own lives, and Sagittarius shows us that our enthusiasm is never frivolous—there is deep truth within the joy.

When it comes to celestial bodies, the most obvious pick is our very own sun, which is literally made of fire. Mars, the red planet, is also associated with the fire element. In astrology, Mars rules our drive, willpower, and how we act, just as fire does in the classical elements.

In tarot, fire is represented by the suit of wands. If you already know a bit about tarot, you may have read that wands represent creativity, but I think that's a one-dimensional view. As we've seen and discussed, creativity is a holistic process that blossoms when we learn the tools that work for us to access our magic. As a society, we tend to use creativity and inspiration interchangeably, when they're two separate things. Inspiration is an occurrence or insight that pushes us to act, while creativity is all of that, plus the unique blend of tools and techniques that we cultivate to hone our process. In my opinion, creativity is a few steps beyond the inspiration part.

All this to say, the meanings beyond the cards are up to you to decide. If you feel like the suit of wands, which is full of depictions of trials and adventures, represents creativity to you, then it does. That's that. For me, though, this suit is all about the internal and external environments we explore to find the spark of divine inspiration.

In nature, our sun casts a golden light over every surface it touches, enveloping us in warmth and heat. It's the transformative energy that allows seeds to unravel beneath the soil, to become the next version of themselves. The fire element is associated with the summer, when the sun is at its most powerful and reminds us that we all deserve a place in the light.

SPELLWORK: FIND YOUR FIRE POWER OBJECT

Just as you've done with the other three elements, you'll go through the same process to uncover the object you'd like to represent fire. Find a fresh page in your notebook, write "Fire" across the top, and give yourself the time and space to sink into this practice. Close your eyes. Imagine inhaling the smoky scent of a bonfire. Let any memories you have of fire waft through your mind. Write down or doodle any ideas that come up.

Once you have an idea of your relationship to the fire element, choose an item that you'll eventually collect. For example, if you have fond memories of playing games with your family around the fire and you associate it with joy and connection, you might choose a piece of a board game or something that makes you smile. Truly, the possibilities are endless.

Other options that typically represent the fire element are "smoky" crystals like smoky quartz or red stones; cinnamon, frankincense, and any other spicy scents; candles of all kinds; and anything that represents the sun.

ETHER: THE MYSTICAL MAGICIAN

There's one final element that any modern magic-maker should familiarize themselves with, and that's ether. Also known as *spirit,* ether is considered the unseen fifth element that animates the other four. It's mystical, mysterious, and can feel a bit untouchable. But the thing about ether is that you always, always know it when you experience it.

It's that sense of wonder when everything aligns in perfect synchronicity. It's that feeling of awe when you witness a breathtaking sunset or shooting stars streaking through the night sky. It's that feeling of being held by a force greater than you, even while you take a running leap into the unknown. I most often recognize ether when I'm at the finish line of a draft, and I'm not quite sure how it'll all work out, only to discover that I had planted all the seeds I needed in the very beginning. That tiny detail I added in the first act, that weapon or outfit or dialogue that I thought was "just for fun"? In the final act, ether reminds me that there are no coincidences and that my creativity and imagination have had some help all along.

In spiritual practices, ether goes by many names. The word for *ether* in ancient yogic practices is the *akash,* and means "space." This is where there is absolute stillness without the influence of the other elements, yet it's within this stillness that all life is born. Ancient alchemists pursued ether with fervor and considered it the secret ingredient to creating gold and other precious metals. In Christianity, ether is represented by the Holy Spirit. In one way or another, ether, or spirit, shows up in some capacity in just about every religion in the world.

Ether also plays an incredibly important role in our definition of magic. As we know, magic is the intersection of chaos and order, and each one of us will have our own unique sweet spot as to how to tap into it and learn its rhythm and texture. Ether is the infinite space where anything and everything is possible, where all potential magics reside. When we tap into our magic, we also work with ether.

At the end of the day, anyone can create anything. That's both the wonder and audacity of this world. But to create something that's authentically *you* requires that you tap into ether to bring forth the parts of yourself that are most tender and true.

THE MAGIC OF ETHER

Ether is a part of every mystical experience in the history of time. It isn't represented by a specific zodiac sign or planet, and it isn't in any single suit in the tarot. It's not a season or structure in nature. Ether is the unseen in-between of everything.

It's represented in the transits and aspects between celestial bodies, the conversations that the planets are constantly having with each other and us. It's also in all of deep space and the hidden planets we've yet to discover in this galaxy and beyond. In tarot, ether shows up as a thread in the journey of each suit and the Major Arcana. It's in the happenstances that get us from one milestone to the next, through the births and rebirths present in each journey. And in nature, it's the first breath of each new season, the lull between moon phases, the sacred pause after a storm.

At its core, ether is more about the experience than it is something that you can get your hands on. We all experience it differently, but when it comes into our awareness, it's hard to blow it off as something else. It's a hitch in your gut when you finally connect the dots in a project you've been working on, the quickening of your heartbeat when you see something or someone that you just know is meant to be in your life.

And, most important, you can only invite ether into your life—not demand it. We do this by becoming conscious of the other elements and how we connect with them and then by creating space for your relationship with them, and yourself, to grow.

SPELLWORK: CREATE YOUR ELEMENTAL ALTAR

If you've had a chance to gather the objects you'll use to represent water, earth, air, and fire, now is the time to create a special spot on your altar for them.

Don't be intimidated by the word *altar*. While organized religion has co-opted the term, an altar is simply a surface where you work with your sacred tools and participate in rituals. And the best part is that your altar can literally be anywhere. Some magic-makers like to have a whole separate table to work with their tools, while others prefer to build their altar into a space where they know they'll spend a lot of time. Personally, I have an extra-long desk that doubles as both my work space and altar. This feels right to me, as I find that I'm most often tapping into my own magic when I'm writing and working in this space.

The reason why we're setting up an elemental altar is twofold. First, there is actually a bit of research to back up why looking at images and objects representing something important to us actu-

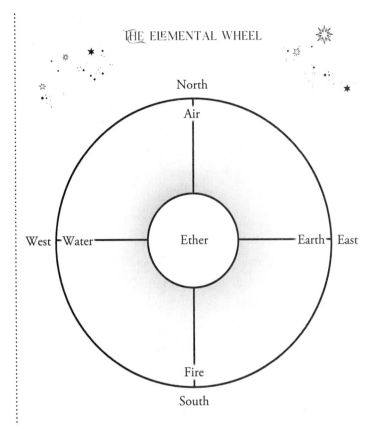

THE ELEMENTAL WHEEL

North

Air

West ⊢Water⊸   Ether   ⊢Earth⊣ East

Fire

South

ally works. According to neuroscience research, the brain naturally does something called *value-tagging,* where it begins to assign importance to things it sees regularly, thus paying attention to thoughts, emotions, and opportunities related to them. By assigning meaning and importance to your elemental objects, and then placing them where you'll view them regularly, you're automatically setting yourself up for magic-making success.

Secondly, everyday objects have been used as amulets and talismans for a millennium. They've been charged with the task of helping the wearer to tap into the mystical to protect, manipulate energy, and work miracles. The practice of whispering wants and wishes into physical objects is as old as humankind, and I have to believe that the practice wouldn't have lasted this long if there were not some benefit to it.

So back to your altar. Once you've decided on your space and have collected your objects, place one at the top of your altar, one at the bottom, one to the left, and one to the right. This should be a wholly intuitive practice—go with your gut on which object should go in which space. If you aren't sure where you'd like to place each object, you can always opt to go with a traditional interpretation of the classical elements and their associated directions, often found on the indigenous medicine wheel.

Just remember: The center of your elemental altar is a sacred space for you to tap into your creative magic. If you're a writer like I am, you may even want to create the circle around where you sit at your desk to write. Or around your latest painting or the space where you play your instrument.

Think of your elemental objects and the circle you create with them as a private space. It's a safety net, a soothing balm, and a chaos-proof room for you to do your creative work. Each time you look at your objects, you'll remember the relationship you're building with each element, as well as different parts of yourself, and focus on the potency of your work. In time, as you have more and more creative successes within this space, your body and mind will be able to slip into "creative mode" with greater ease each time you sit down to make. And if that isn't magic in action, I don't know what is.

7

ASTROLOGY

BEFORE WE DIVE into this chapter, take a moment to consider every blog post, article, social media post, and text from your friends that had something to do with astrology . . . in the past week. There was a time when your answer may have been "zero," but if you're someone who spends even a small portion of your time online, chances are you've encountered some pop astrology content in the past several days.

There are a lot of reasons why astrology has flooded mainstream media in full force over the past few years. Practicing astrologers will point to a variety of patterns and planetary transits that have opened up another wave of spiritualism, but truly, the planet most responsible for this increased interest is Earth. It's *hard* living here, y'all, especially if you're the highly sensitive, creative type. We're smack-dab in the middle of a huge, global transition between the old ways of doing things (ahem, patriarchy) and a broader, more equitable way of being, but we've got a long way to go yet. Add to that the looming climate crisis and crumbling institutions, and we end up with a whole lot of people trying to make sense of why they're here, on this planet, by looking to the sky at what else is out there.

It's not like this sacred tool is new. Astrology, in some form, has been around for twenty-five thousand years, with humans tracking lunar cycles with bones and paintings on cave walls. Like any good tool, it has evolved and continues to evolve as we do, much like language does. There are Eastern and Western genres of astrology and dozens of branches within each. There are branches of astrology that focus on personal relationships, ones that explore specific dates in history, and others that read the planetary patterns of current events. I work within the realm of natal astrology, which analyzes strengths and lessons according to your placements at birth, and psychological astrology, which views each celestial body as an aspect of your personality and behavior. And because astrology is a tool that grows and changes as we do, I also blend my own special brand of magic and creativity into my practice.

Please know that the following explanations, archetypes, and methods are based on my personal astrology practice. As you're reading through, sit with the information and decide if it resonates with you. If it doesn't, that's *completely okay*. It also doesn't mean you should throw astrology out as a possible tool altogether. There just may be another branch or even astrologer out there that you vibe with more. The only goal is to keep an open mind going in.

THE ZODIAC WHEEL

If you were ready to delve into your sun sign, I have some news for you: that's not even the most important part of astrology. I know, I know. It's frustrating, right? We've built our entire personalities around being a fiery Aries or tender Cancer, when our sun sign is such a small part of the overall picture. And while I love a good pop astrology meme, it can also really distort our viewpoint of both ourselves and what astrology actually *is*.

Like most magical tools, astrology helps us to see something—whether it's our behavior, the past, or the big picture—from a unique perspective. It's a tool that's best explained as a full circle of possibilities instead of within the context of a single sign.

This is where we bring in the most important tool for using astrology: the zodiac wheel.

The zodiac wheel is a visual representation of all twelve constellations in the sky and the order in which they occur from our viewpoint here on Earth. These constellations represent a myth, or a poignant story that's been woven into the tapestry of our history to help us make sense of the human experience. Through these stories, the zodiac signs and their archetypes and traits were born. The wheel also depicts the horizon line, cutting our circle in half through the middle. This horizon line is super important and will come into play as you're working with your own chart.

Here is a secret about astrology that isn't in the memes:

ZODIAC WHEEL

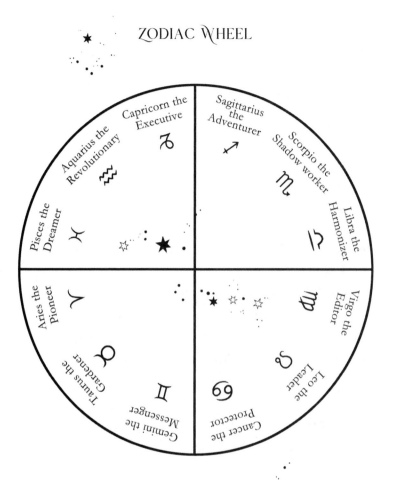

Every single zodiac sign is a part of your cosmic blueprint. That's right; while you may be adamant that you have big-boss Capricorn energy, you *also* have dreamy Pisces and sociable Gemini and intense Scorpio that represent parts of you, too. You know what else that means? I hate to say it, but if there's a sign you absolutely can't stand, it's probably time to take a closer look in the mirror to figure out what traits associated with that sign you're uncomfortable with in yourself.

This image of the general zodiac wheel is what's considered a "natural chart," meaning it begins with Aries, the first sign in the zodiac, touching up against the underside of that horizon line. It then moves counterclockwise through the rest of the signs as it continues with Taurus, Gemini, Cancer, and so on, until it loops back around to the twelfth and final sign, Pisces, which touches the horizon line from the opposite side. The wheel then begins all over again.

Just like each individual constellation and sign is associated with a myth, all twelve of the signs in their natural order take us through a journey of self-realization, from the raw warrior energy of Aries as we first step into the world to the healing and endings associated with Pisces.

A JOURNEY THROUGH THE SIGNS

ARIES: THE PIONEER

As the "youngest" sign of the zodiac, the Aries archetype is naturally fearless. This energy possesses a childlike innocence that believes anything is possible, and people with a lot of Aries in their chart tend to revel in the energy of new beginnings. As the first sign on the wheel, Aries is responsible for not only ushering in its specific season but acts as a catalyst for the entire journey. A warrior at heart, Aries reminds us to be brave in pursuit of our dreams.

Taurus: The Gardener

Once we get a push forward on our journey from Aries, Taurus helps to stabilize us in our new world. Everything slows down when we step into the threshold of Taurus energy, and we turn our attention to the fine details that need to be taken care of to continue forward. It's one thing to burst forth onto the scene and another to harness that energy to gather the resources and supplies you'll need to continue onward without burning yourself out. Like a master gardener, the Taurus archetype steadfastly tills the soil to nurture important resources.

Gemini: The Messenger

There are always surprises on any journey, and Gemini is ready to take them on with the full force of their wit and charm. The Gemini archetype is flexible, fluid, and insatiably curious, which makes it that much easier for those with planets in this sign to use their intellectual and social resources to bypass any obstacles in the road. Gemini energy is all about the duality of idea development, or the push-pull between expression and reception, creating and thinking, as we figure out the message we're trying to convey.

Cancer: The Protector

If there's one archetype that's most misunderstood, it's Cancer. Traditionally known as a soft-spoken nurturer, people with planets in this sign can feel stifled by the old-school, matriarchal vision of Cancer. But truly, at its core, the Cancer archetype urges us to remember that our home expands outside of our own wants, needs, and immediate community. Feeling safe and stable in our lives also requires that *others* feel safe in theirs, too, and that sense of security is worth protecting. There can be no peace in our city, country, or world until we work to ensure that we all have our own sense of sanctuary. In a natural chart, Cancer falls at the very bottom, representing the "basement" of our subconscious, or the foundation from upon which we create.

LEO: THE LEADER

As we come into contact with more people and possibilities on our path forward, it becomes more important than ever to reestablish our own inner truth. This is where the Leo archetype shines. Ruled by the heart, Leo energy reminds us that when we tap into our deepest truths and honor them for what they are, we can move forward with confidence and courage. Lionhearted Leo also reminds us that joy and pleasure have an integral role to play in the creative process. All those playlists, aesthetic boards, and fan art act as inspiration fuel when a project seems daunting.

VIRGO: THE EDITOR

While Leo reminds us that creating should feel good, Virgo tells us when it's time to get to work. Ever the efficient analyzer, the Virgo archetype calls us to tune back in to the fine details we need to address, like what our day-to-day schedule looks like, how to manage our time, and how to stay healthy so we can create. More than any other sign, Virgo understands how to cut away the excess to lighten the load so we can move forward with less friction.

LIBRA: THE HARMONIZER

As we shift into the second half of our journey and the second half of the zodiac wheel, Libra shows us that the path is made so much easier in partnership. As the harmonizer of the zodiac, Libra energy reminds us that the journey was never just for our own actualization; we were always meant to include others so that we can support them while they also support us, in perfect symbiosis, just as Libra likes it. From Libra to Pisces, the second half of the wheel takes our art from private to public, personal to interpersonal.

SCORPIO: THE SHADOW WORKER

As we build relationships, we can expand our capacity to hold space for magic by merging with another. This is the realm of shadow worker Scorpio, which teaches us that becoming intimate with yourself or another is not always rainbows and puppies. In fact, it *can't* be. To really know yourself, your art, and others, you have to be willing to traverse the shadow. This is the part of the process where our closest confidantes can show us the parts of our project that still need work, or even parts of ourselves we've been unwilling to look at. By walking through the darkness, we build our ability to hold on to the light.

SAGITTARIUS: THE ADVENTURER

If there is ever a sign that isn't satisfied by the status quo, it's Sagittarius. This adventurer never stops expanding their horizons, whether that's through travel, education, or publishing through the media. Now that we've had the chance to experience intimacy with Scorpio, the Sagittarius archetype encourages us to apply this new transformative, soul-opening knowledge to shape our philosophy on how the world works. This energy calls for a leap of faith, whether that looks like selling your work or putting it in a drawer, knowing that you can try it all over again.

CAPRICORN: THE EXECUTIVE

Sitting at the very top of the zodiac wheel is Capricorn, right where this archetype belongs. This archetype understands that all the knowledge gained thus far on the journey is meant to be translated into the bigger structures and systems of society to keep it humming along. At the same time, Capricorn energy at its most evolved is also willing to rebuild systems that aren't working for *everyone* in pursuit of streamlining society at its most foundational level. Capricorn energy represents a culmination point, which could look like the sale or publication of a project, sharing it with a close group, or framing it and placing it in your home.

AQUARIUS: THE REVOLUTIONARY

Sometimes, even the most aggressive tweaks to current systems won't get the job done. This is where radical Aquarius enters the equation. This innovative energy ushers in sudden change, breaking down the barrier to our own collective genius in the process. Aquarius energy is far-reaching and visionary and has the talent for tapping into the possibility of what *could* be, if only we were willing to reach that high. Tapping into Aquarius energy is embracing the future and all its possibilities. This the part of the process where you can start to connect the dots between where you're going, your long-term dreams, and the next thing that longs to be made through you.

PISCES: THE DREAMER

There's a lot to be said for dreams, and mystical Pisces knows how to navigate these ethereal waters with ease. As the final sign on the zodiac wheel, this archetype is responsible for ushering in the energy of healing so that we can dream a new version of ourselves into being. We have been through so much on this journey, but we still must pause to stitch up our battle wounds before we begin on our next adventure. Pisces reminds us that rest is essential to the integration of our lessons. This way, we don't make the same mistakes as we begin our next journey around the wheel.

THE NATAL CHART: YOUR PERSONAL ZODIAC WHEEL

Each and every one of us has our very own personal zodiac wheel that takes us on a journey through the twelve signs. Our own wheel—also called our natal, or birth, chart—acts as the backdrop to the story the planets were playing out at the exact moment of our birth. When we begin to examine how the planets, houses, and even the elements show up to tell the story of our potential, purpose, and pitfalls, our chart becomes a powerful and insightful tool.

Your natal chart may look a lot like the "natural wheel" we've been discussing, or you may find that the signs in your chart don't line up the same way. For example, your chart may start with Aquarius (or any other sign) just beneath the horizon line instead of Aries. All that means is that a constellation other than Aries was on the eastern horizon at the moment of your birth. This is determined by the exact time you were born.

If right about now you're wondering how the birthplace, date, and time could possibly generate such a potent tool into knowing yourself and your creative process, you aren't alone. It can be difficult to wrap our minds around how the alignment of the planets could possibly have any influence over who we are now and who we're becoming. While I wish I could give you a definitive explanation on *why* astrology works, I can't do that. All I know is that it *does* work. I've seen it work for me, my students, and my clients a million times over.

Some ancient astrologers believed that the human soul comes directly from the universe, and as it wafts down from the cosmos, it passes through each planet, picking up its energy, before manifesting on Earth. Others believe that the soul chooses the exact moment to be born so as to leverage the strengths and pitfalls of their cosmic blueprint so they can learn important evolutionary lessons in this lifetime. Some believe it's the sacred geometry in the aspects between the planets or the myths we've collected imprinted on the stars that lend to magic.

There may be some truth in all of those theories, but astrology resonates with me and many creatives because of a far earthlier reason. We may be ethereal souls, but we have a very human body that responds and resonates with patterns, cycles, and seasons. Our connection to Earth lends itself to understand how there is also a bigger, broader pattern at play, and there's a part of us that is responding to much larger and more universal cycles at the same time we're also reawakening for spring or preparing for slumber in the winter. We are part of nature, and the cosmos is *also* part of nature.

As creatives, our hearts and minds are often doing double time, even as we go about our day-to-day lives. I know for me, personally, I am simultaneously tending to the mundane routines in my home, while also writing to meet deadlines, while also planning my next projects, *while also* allowing my mind to explore the seed of a new idea before I fall asleep each night. I'm here on Earth at the same time my mind is taking a lap around the galaxy. Just as we can and should simultaneously pay attention to the changing seasons while also considering Pluto's shift into a new sign after a decades-long transit. We contain multitudes, after all.

At the very least, we can look at our natal chart as an interesting storytelling tool that provides us with the language to understand ourselves. The great thing about astrology is that you don't have to believe in all of it—or any of it, really—to use this tool. Just consider it with an open mind and go from there. You never know what new information you may glean about yourself just by looking at a map of the stars.

To start to use our chart as a tool, we'll explore three essential keys to getting to know your cosmic blueprint and how you can use it to inform your creativity. But first, you'll need to generate your natal chart.

Spellwork: Generate Your Natal Chart

There are tons of places online where you can pull up your natal chart for free. One of the most comprehensive sources that many experts recommend is www.astro.com, under the "Horoscope" section. If you're looking for a clean-line chart that's simpler, you could also try www.astro-charts.com. To generate your chart, you'll need your birth date, location of birth, and exact birth time.

And yes, the exact time really does matter! The rising sign (also called the *ascendant*) changes about every two hours, which means if your birth time is off by even an hour, your rising sign could be inaccurate. And *that* means your entire chart would be inaccurate because it's the ascendant that sets up the position of the houses. The moon also shifts signs about every two and a half days. If you were born on a day when the moon transitioned from one sign to the next, there's a chance you could have the wrong moon sign if you don't have your correct birth time.

For an extreme example of this, my daughter was born two minutes after the moon shifted into Libra. If I would have been even two minutes off, she'd be considered an earthy Virgo moon instead of the highly fashionable Libra moon that this little queen is. Even a couple of minutes makes a difference in astrology.

When you have your chart wheel, save or print it. We'll be looking at it in length in the next section.

• •

WHAT IF I DON'T KNOW MY BIRTH TIME?

If you can't locate your birth time, you still have some options. You can set your birth time to 12:00 p.m. for the time zone in which you were born, but please know that you'll need to focus on the planets and their signs instead of the house system, as you can't be sure it's correct. Another option is to set your birth time as the time of sunrise on your birthday. (Fun fact: This is how most pop astrology is set up since we all know our birthdays and can identify with our sun signs.) Just search for the time of sunrise on your birthday, then put that into the chart generator. Just know that, again, your house system may be incorrect. Finally, if you're dead set on knowing your chart through and through, you can hire an astrologer who specializes in chart rectification to help you out.

KEY #1: THE ELEMENTS

Yep, we're back at it with the elements again. As mentioned in the previous chapter, the elements show up in the sky, too, and there's plenty we can learn from them within our natal chart. As we know, there's a trio of zodiac signs that is ruled by one of the four classical elements: water, earth, air, and fire. When we have planets that fall within an element, it's like there's an extra concentration of energy there, and it's important that we pay close attention to it. As you're first getting to know your natal chart, it's easier to look at the story it tells as a whole, including the elements you have in abundance or may be lacking, instead of focusing in on a sign in particular.

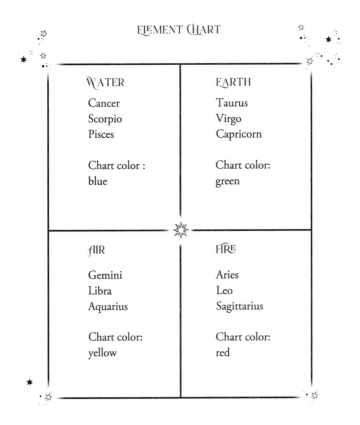

ELEMENT CHART

WATER
Cancer
Scorpio
Pisces

Chart color :
blue

EARTH
Taurus
Virgo
Capricorn

Chart color:
green

AIR
Gemini
Libra
Aquarius

Chart color:
yellow

FIRE
Aries
Leo
Sagittarius

Chart color:
red

Think of the signs as a certain flavor of each element. For example, all fire signs may be spicy, but Aries is habanero sauce, Leo is red pepper flakes, and Sagittarius is smoky barbecue. When you learn the basic elements that rule your chart first, it's much easier to get the overall "flavor" of your chart, which is easier to understand. Then you can distinguish those flavors and tune in to the fine details later.

Take a look at the natal chart you've generated and look for the elements. Some sites will list the number of planets you have stationed in each element in a chart off to the side, while others will require a bit of digging on your part. If you don't see an elemental breakdown on your chart, go through each planet and identify which sign it's in. Most, if not all, free charts will color-code the elements for you as well so you can get a better picture. Here's a quick synopsis of how to identify the elements in your chart.

Go ahead and search for each planet. If you see that Mercury is in Libra, for example, you know that it's in an air sign. Mark a tally down for "air" in your notebook. Keep going until you have all the planets, celestial bodies, and important points covered.

Now let's take a look at what you've got.

In most cases, you'll have a stronger pull in one or two elements over the others, yet still have a couple of planets or placements in each element. That being said, I've seen charts that are very heavy in a single element and others that are completely balanced across all four. Whatever comes up for you and your chart, spend a minute considering what you've learned about the elements thus far. If you discovered that you have a lot of earth energy in your chart, do you also relate to some of the attributes of earth—steady, detail-oriented, and determined?

Perhaps you'll answer no to that question, and that's fine. Remember: Defining the elements in your chart is only one key to unlocking your creative process. A natal chart is so chock-full of information that we're never truly done learning from it, no matter how many times we interpret it.

Balancing and Complementing the Elements

Let's say you *do* identify with earth energy. You're steadfast, loyal, and like to work methodically. You have an abundance of earth energy in your natal chart, and you're great at getting through your to-do list, but when it comes to following the spark of spontaneous inspiration, you struggle a bit. In fact, you're looking for a way to add more joy back to your creative life by remembering how much fun it can be to follow your excitement.

In this case, you'll want to look at bringing your strong earth vibes into balance so you can access the other elements in your chart. You may also want to consider encouraging the fire element in your chart to speak a little louder while you're on the hunt for joy and inspiration. And remember: Just like we have all twelve zodiac signs in our chart, we also have access to all four elements. It just may take us a bit more effort to bring one element on line more than the others. Fortunately, we can *all* do this kind of magic-making, no matter what our natal chart looks like.

WATER

We know that water is fluid, flexible, and speaks in the language of emotions. In the creative process, it represents the feelings and emotions we pour into our projects. Often when we're stuck, it's because we've built up a dam inside us that hasn't allowed for exploration of our wounds. Similarly in our natal chart, planets in the water element require us to tap into our emotions and intuition to access their magic. It takes courage to open yourself up in this way, but only when we feel to our greatest depths can we also touch the hearts of those who engage with our work. And that's the goal of art, isn't it? To remind us all what it means to be human through tenderness and feeling.

To amplify: If you have little or no water in your natal chart, or you find yourself stuck on a project or afraid to move forward, tap into water energy to get into flow again. Some suggestions are yin or restorative yoga, yoga nidra, meditation, music with soulful lyrics that touch your heart, reading poetry and letting it simmer, tapping into your intuition through water or mirror scrying, essential oil baths, and literally taking a swim.

To soften: On the other hand, if you have a ton of water energy in your chart, or you're feeling too overwhelmed by your emotions to work on your art, you'll want to look to water's complementary element: earth. Feel your feelings, for sure, but allow earth energy to provide you with stability and structure so you can get the work done, too. Set yourself up with blocks of time to journal and release your emotions in a safe space, then focus on the details of your project. Just knowing that you have the time and space to process your emotions can allow you to turn your attention to the less fluid details of making art.

WATER SIGN ASTRO TIPS

Cancer: To stabilize Cancer energy, *sanctuary* is your key word. No matter where you create, try to make your physical space soulful and inviting, and most important, safe. If that means putting a lock on the door to your office so you can sort through your emotions unencumbered, then by all means, head to the hardware store ASAP.

Scorpio: Scorpio energy requires depth to feel fulfilled, so carving out blocks of time for just *being* is a must. More than anything, people with many planets in this sign have to find a way to explore their rich inner landscape to sort through and unearth all the information there. Solitude will always be a boon to a Scorpio's creative endeavors.

Pisces: Dreamy Pisces is the ocean that connects us all. People with a lot of Pisces energy can work their special brand of magic once they've had an adequate amount of rest. Resting allows this sign to recalibrate and sort through all the information and emotions they pick up from others all day, every day, to figure out what's truly theirs to hold on to so they can create from a place of authenticity.

EARTH

Every project requires structure to bring it into form, and that's where earth comes in. All the time we spend organizing, outlining, and setting up the bones of a project is considered earth energy—the very foundation from which our project seeds grow. If we feel like we're constantly turning our wheels and not making much progress in our craft, it could be because we need to go back and reset the foundation. That may include taking classes and working with critique partners, or it could involve setting up a disciplined schedule that you try to adhere to. While it may not be the dreamiest idea, it's the commitment that follows the inspiration that gets the work done.

To amplify: If you have little to no earth energy in your chart or you feel like you're spinning your wheels and can't figure out the next steps to take, you may need to work more consciously with earth energy to build the structures that can help you finish your project. Some suggestions include strength-training exercise, hiking and spending time in nature, collecting rocks, making crystal grids, massage, gardening or tending to plants and pets, grounding meditations, and adorning your work space with items and textures that engage your physical senses.

To soften: Earth energy is great until you become a bit too rigid—and your creativity suffers for it. To tamp down on the earth energy so you can let your magic flow, look to the activities that amplify water. Other options also include taking a quick break from your project to create something just for you, just for fun, and try writing or creating in a different style or medium to break out of patterns of rigidity.

Earth Sign Astro Tips

Taurus: As the first earth sign on the zodiac wheel, Taurus requires a solid foundation from which to launch their dreams.

This archetype isn't always comfortable with change, so creating a routine on which you can rely will help anyone with a lot of Taurus energy in their chart feel at ease. Bonus points if you build in time for a little luxury, too, as earthy Taurus loves to indulge in the senses.

Virgo: Virgo energy prefers efficiency, and it's never easier to tap into this sign's strengths than when taking care of your mind and body. Creating meals and digging up snacks that help your body feel good, while also taking mental breaks for meditation and just, you know, *resting,* will help prevent your nervous system from going into overdrive.

Capricorn: No one loves to climb like a determined Capricorn. Embrace that ambitious energy and build in weekly space to strategize. There's nothing that dampens this archetype quicker than only dealing with monotonous day-to-day tasks, so if you have a lot of planets in Capricorn, be sure to give yourself time and space to plan your quarters and years.

AIR

Even the most passionate pursuits need a dash of logic. Bringing in and balancing air energy in your chart can help you to clearly see the dots you need to connect to make a project shine. That may look like plot threads you've let hang loose, or dynamics between characters in your manuscript, or small snippets of a chorus that still needs a verse or two. If you don't have much air energy in your chart, you may find that following your curiosity or making essential connections between thoughts and ideas is difficult. That said, tons of air energy tends to lend itself to an over-flexibility, so much so that we can sweep up thoughts that belong to others, only to be disappointed later when they don't align with our vision.

To amplify: Amping up air energy can help create space so you can think clearly about your project. And with more space and laser-sharp focus comes a clearer vision of your art *and* how to get to the final product. Some suggestions to amp up air energy include joining or creating a small community for socialization and accountability, defining the overall theme of a project and then "connecting the dots" between sections or milestones, working on logic puzzles, learning something new, flexibility exercises, burning incense, and literally opening up the windows for fresh air.

To soften: Too much air energy can be taxing on the nervous system. With so many thoughts flitting about, it can also be difficult to discern which ideas to follow into flow and which you should let go of. To soften air energy, consider cutting back on stimulants, sitting or placing your feet on the earth for stability, disconnecting from apps, email, and your phone for the day, relying on a steady and familiar routine, and breathing exercises to calm and slow the heart rate.

Air Sign Astro Tips

Gemini: This sociable archetype is at its best when it has access to fresh ideas and people to run them by. To tap into this ebullient energy, connect with others, either online or in real life, and engage in nourishing conversation. You may be surprised how another's viewpoint can trigger a brilliant new idea.

Libra: There's no better way to soothe Libra than with a visually pleasing environment. Think: interesting artwork, a harmonious color palette, and perfectly placed knickknacks. Libra also prefers harmony in *all* aspects of life and enjoys a balanced approach to creative pursuits. To balance an abundance of Libra energy, consider what parts of yourself and your projects you're ready to share with those closest to you, and which parts are just for you and you alone.

Aquarius: As the visionary of the zodiac, Aquarius energy can see the broader picture of how all the pieces come together to affect the collective. Aquarius energy needs plenty of space to put all their thoughts in order, so be sure to create chunks of time in your schedule to sit, process, and listen. Aquarius also loves to innovate. Letting your mind go all the way outside of the box, even if nothing comes of your invention, will feel thrilling and nourishing.

FIRE

You can usually sense a person with a fire-heavy chart from your first meeting. A lot of fire in a chart can lend itself to someone who's warm, passionate, and willing to hop on opportunities as soon as a glimmer of inspiration appears on their mental horizon. Abundant fire energy lends itself to passion for your projects, motivation to hit the ground running . . . and a tendency to barrel through, even at your own detriment. Lack of fire energy, on the other hand, can show its face as fear of making any decisions and moving forward, or difficulty uncovering what inspires you and your work.

To amplify: Fire energy is all about movement, inspiration, and transformation. Adding more fire energy in your process can help you rediscover *why* you want to do this work in the first place—especially if you've been struggling with motivation. It can also inspire you to move forward with gusto and unbridled optimism. To increase fire energy, some options include cardio exercise, dancing, fire or bonfire scrying, burning candles, sunbathing, belly laughing, playing games and doing crafts just for pleasure and fun, going on a spontaneous adventure, taking the first actionable step toward a big dream, and anything else that gets your heart pumping.

To soften: On the other hand, if you're someone who has a lot of fire energy in your chart, you may find that it's easy to get started on your project, but the propensity for burnout is real. Plus, it may be difficult to stick to an established routine, and you may only want to create when you feel inspired. To balance and soften some of this fiery energy, some options include gentle yin yoga to release excess fire energy, full-body-scan meditation, alternate nostril breathing exercises, and "brain dumping" all your inspired ideas into a journal or digital space so you can analyze them from a logical perspective later.

Fire Sign Astro Tips

Aries: *Movement* is the key word for highly motivated Aries. As the first sign on the natural zodiac wheel, Aries energy is at its most productive (and way less self-destructive) when you can direct it into a challenge or competition, even if it's just you versus you. Set yourself up with a challenge to complete a section of your project within a certain amount of time, and be sure to allow for plenty of breaks for walks and other forms of physical movement.

Leo: As the heart-driven leader of the zodiac, Leo energy is best directed toward joy, play, and the indulgences that light you up from the inside out. From this place of pleasure, you can access your highest peak of inspiration—and remember why you chose to create in the first place. Make a game of your creative process, while also taking time to play just for play's sake.

Sagittarius: As the cosmic truth-seeker, the Sagittarius archetype prefers to pour energy into projects that expand the horizons of your own mind and the mind of anyone who absorbs your art. With an abundance of Sagittarius energy in your chart, you'll want to give yourself a hearty push outside of your comfort zone. Explore a new genre, work within a new medium, and go further than you ever dreamed you could.

SPELLWORK: CONSIDER YOUR ASTRO ELEMENTAL MAKEUP

In your notebook, write down your astro elemental makeup. This will include the number of planets, points, and celestial bodies you have in each of the four elements. This doesn't have to be complicated! You could keep it simple by jotting down the name of each element, followed by the number of planets you have in each one. Working with sacred tools really can be that easy. We'll use this information in the following sections as we break down the planets in your chart to give you a solid overview of your cosmic blueprint.

KEY #2: PLANETARY POWER

Once you've figured out your elemental makeup, the next key to unlocking your natal chart involves taking a closer look at the planets. We've already established which planets fall in which elements, but now we'll get to know each of them on a more personal level.

Note that many astrologers use the term *planets* to describe the main celestial bodies in our solar system, even though the sun, moon, and Chiron are not planets. The sun and moon are considered luminaries, and Chiron is currently classified as a comet, but is sometimes also called a minor planet. For the purpose of simplicity, the term *planets* is used as a collective noun when grouping all the celestial bodies we read together.

Okay, that's that. Now on to the good stuff.

Here's another secret about astrology: it's really all about the planets. We tend to think in terms of the zodiac when we think of astrology, but in truth, it's about listening to and learning the language of each planet. Astrologers are really just cosmic eavesdroppers, pressing our ears to the edges of the universe while we listen to the planets whisper to each other across time and space. The element a planet is in simply informs its basic disposition, and its zodiac sign further emphasizes the "flavor" in which each planet expresses itself.

INTERPRETING THE PLANETS

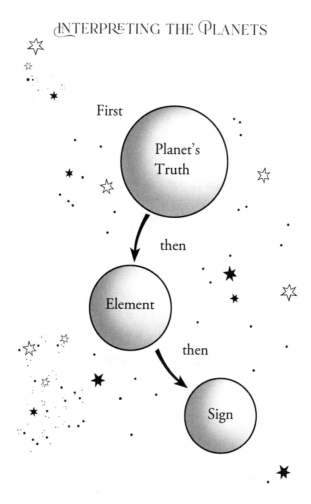

First

Planet's
Truth

then

Element

then

Sign

Take Venus, for example. In Western astrology, Venus represents what we love and value, no matter which element or zodiac sign it falls in. That is this planet's truth. If your Venus is in an air sign, its basic disposition is communicative and quick-thinking. And let's take it one step further: if it's in Gemini, it tends to express its love through talking and writing, and it values connection through sharing thoughts and ideas.

In the following sections, we'll take a look at each celestial body and how their truth speaks to the creative process. When we understand each planet's meaning and can see the connection between its cycles and our own personal creativity cycle, we can leverage this self-knowledge to flow and create in sync with the universe instead of working against it.

THE INNER PLANETS: YOUR DAY-TO-DAY GUIDE TO SUCCESS

The closer the celestial body is to Earth, the greater influence it has on us personally. This is why the inner planets have the biggest say in our daily happenstances and routines—including our creative process. When we get to know each of the planets and our two luminaries, the sun and moon, and learn how they speak to us through our charts, we can change how we make art for the better.

THE SUN

Each night, our sun traverses through the underworld and crests the eastern horizon once again, flooding our planet with warmth and light. Not only does the sun help to regulate our rest cycle, but it's also the literal and metaphoric fire power needed to encourage growth. It warms the soil, coaxing seeds from their shells, and signifies the passing of days, weeks, and months, reminding us that we, too, are always growing. In Western astrology, the sun typically represents how *you* shine. It's also attributed to your purpose, on this planet, in this lifetime.

That's a heavy burden to bear, isn't it? The concept of *purpose* has become so convoluted as more and more esoteric practices enter into mainstream culture. Our purpose is supposed to be our reason for living, for even *existing*. It's supposed to signify a deep-rooted love of the work you do, and when you find it, you're expected to enjoy every last breath while you engage with it. And forget about compensation; you don't need to worry about money when you're living your purpose. No pressure, right?

This is the natural consequence of distilling ancient wisdom into a bite-size snippet for capitalist consumption. We also have to consider *who* are the people that control the books, media, and online publications that print our monthly horoscopes. At the end of the day, does it benefit the people at the top for us all to fret over our purpose according to our sun sign, including feeling shame over wanting fair compensation for the work we do? It's a lot to consider, honestly. And I don't even want to get started about the sun being a symbol of masculine energy and how its importance has been overplayed in pop astrology instead of focusing on extremely profound, yet quieter, planets like the moon and Venus. That's a whole other book.

But what's especially wonderful about a sacred tool like astrology is that it continues to grow, change, and take on new meaning as we grow, too. So let's begin to consider the sun in a new light (pun intended). Let's consider it as *one* part of our inherent creativity and not necessarily the end all, be all of who we are.

When we are thinking about astrology as a holistic system that unlocks our creativity, I consider the sun to be the signifier of what *warms you from the inside out*. It's identified as a feeling more than a thought or the piecing together of how your purpose can support you in the utterly impossible puzzle of capitalism. When we're talking about soulful creativity, the sun represents whatever it is that makes you feel the most like *you* when you're engaged with it.

Of course, this can apply to anyone—not only creatives. But for the purpose of this book, let's consider the activities and projects that warm you, that make you feel *alive*. And the best part is that *there is room to grow* with this new understanding of the sun in astrology. As you change, your projects and interests will change, and what warms you will also change. That is exactly as it should be. When you tap into the truth of your sun, you learn what inspires you on an authentic level, which in turn continues to fuel your work from a deeper, more sustainable source instead of the false rewards of attention, publicity, and admirers. And look, I'll be the first to tell you that there's nothing wrong with wanting those things, but they can't be the main source of inspiration for creating. You will never feel satisfied with your work, for one, and it's much harder to appreciate the creative process, which is extremely internal and personal, when you're only waiting for the accolades to come rolling in.

To access the magic of your sun requires an unraveling of sorts. You'll want to read up on your sun sign (and the house it's in, but more on that later). From there, dig deeper. Let go of any part of a description that doesn't resonate with you and keep digging. With a sacred tool that has gone mainstream, like astrology, you'll have to sort through the myriad of information to get to the essence of what a sun sign really means. To help you out, reread the previous section on the signs and ask yourself: *Is there truth to uncover here?*

THE MOON

If there's a luminary that's doing some heavy lifting in our charts, it's our moon. Unlike other planets, Earth only has one moon to reflect back to us our sunlight—and our own light. It's a tall order, and as the quieter and less flashy of the two luminaries, the moon doesn't get nearly enough attention in mainstream astrology (although that is beginning to change).

As the closest celestial body to Earth, our moon is responsible for reflecting back to us the vibrancy of our sun and helping us to make sense of and leverage that light while living on Earth. It's most often known as the body that gives insight into our emotional undercurrents, can represent intuition and deep-seated feelings, and can help us understand the ebbs and flows of our longings and cravings.

What many people may not know is that the moon is actually a bit earthier than we give it credit for. As the moon doesn't have its own source of light, it can only shine by reflecting sunlight off its craterous surface. Essentially, it shows us how to move within the moment to work with that spiritual glow that warms us. And since we are human beings with a very real skin suit that we have to haul around, care for, and nourish so that we can even feel that inner warmth, the moon also represents our physical bodies. By constantly waxing and waning and shifting into a new zodiac sign every two to three days, our moon gently reminds us that making that inner glow manifest in your life requires adaptability and the willingness to tend to the tides of your emotions and physical body.

When it comes to our creativity, the moon signifies *our entire body of work.* Think of it like this: If you are someone who has invested yourself in a myriad of creative pursuits, whether you completed them all or never finished a single one, the moon gives hints as to how you translated that inner warmth, or inspiration, from your sun into your projects. Perhaps that looks like a body of work that includes picture book ideas, chapter book manuscripts, teaching art classes to toddlers at your church, and maybe even having your own children. If your sun told you that your inner warmth is activated by creating for and with children, then your moon helped you to express it in your daily life by delivering intuitive hits, emotional swells, and physical sensations in the body to let you know which projects to pursue. All in all, without the work of the moon, creating anything that nourishes us from the inside out would be nearly impossible.

There are so many different ways to work with both your natal moon and the transiting moon, but the most potent methods require a distillation of sorts. The moon wants us to understand and put to use our inspiration. By studying its monthly journey through each of the signs, we can best access the wisdom of each phase and address our work. For example, if you observe that the moon is currently in the sign of Libra, you can distill this information into a call for harmony and then build harmony into your process, whether that looks like syncing up with creative friends for a brainstorming session or working with complementary color palettes. This also goes for your natal moon. If you discover that your natal moon is in Taurus, for example, you can distill that information down to this: Taurus thrives in the realm of the physical senses. Translating that to your creative process, you can then create a soothing environment to work in, light candles before you create, and so on. The possibilities of working with the moon are endless and tend to be very personal to the magic-maker.

MERCURY

Never more than twenty-eight degrees from the sun, Mercury shows us how to speak from the center of our inner glow when it's at its best. This tiny, quicksilver planet takes a lap around the zodiac more or less in time with the sun, spending about three weeks in each sign before jetting into the next. As the planet of expression, learning, and listening, Mercury's rapid pace shows us that communicating our message can be as simple and pleasant as we make it, especially when we're speaking from the center of our truth.

If you're a writer, you may already know a bit about Mercury. It's become in vogue to discuss Mercury retrogrades, when the planet appears to be back-spinning through the sky, during the three to four retrograde periods that occur in a single calendar year. It makes sense, really. Mercury is our planet of communication, and when it's not up to full capacity during a retrograde, writers and others who work with words tend to feel the effects most. (At the very least, it's kind of nice to be able to blame writer's block on the cosmos every once in a while.)

That said, I think it's important to realize that Mercury

rules expression *and* listening. While we may not be at our most eloquent when Mercury is off line, that means we should double down on our listening skills instead. Personally, I view retrograde periods as opportunities to quiet external chatter and move even closer to that feeling of warmth. It's a period to reevaluate all the communication we've put out into the world to see if it still aligns with that soulful glow we get from our sun. It's a time of assessment, silence, and communicating with *ourselves* privately, and let's be honest, we don't really value this type of work as a society. We're expected to go, go, go and always be producing, promoting, and sharing. Going retrograde in our own lives tends to insinuate that something is wrong, or that we've run out of good ideas. In truth, we all *need* to go retrograde once in a while to catch our breaths, reconnect with our inspirations, and ensure that we're speaking our truths to power.

This is never more important than it is for someone who wants to share their creations with others. It doesn't matter if you plan to share your pottery with only your best friend, or if you want to publish a book that you hope will touch people all over the world; there's great responsibility in the messages you deliver through your work. Of course making art can and should be pleasurable, but it's also important to remember that once your creation is consumed by others, they are essentially taking in the message sewn into the fabric of your project or product. In creativity, Mercury still serves as our representative of communication, but it has added weight in the chart of anyone who wants to share a message with an audience, no matter the size. I'm going to go out on a limb here and guess that most of us want to share at least a part of our work with *someone,* whether it's your partner or the public at large. Sharing your work, whether it's at an open mic night or anonymously on a forum, requires an added level of care and consideration when working with Mercury's magic.

To work with Mercury, you'll need to get to know all the ways in which you communicate, starting with your internal thoughts and dialogue and moving outward. Meditation is a great starting point to observe your thought patterns. Then, when you're ready, write them down, unfiltered. Similar to the "Scratch It Out" spellwork, cross out thoughts that aren't doing you any favors. This is an ongoing practice (I'm *still* working on being kinder to myself in my head), but as your internal dialogue shifts, you'll find that your outward expression becomes kinder and more dynamic and optimistic, too. We also begin to communicate with crystal clarity in our work, which is the essence of Mercury's magic.

VENUS

You may already be familiar with Venus, at least in name only. Traditionally known as the planet of love, beauty, and desire, Western astrology has long associated it with "feminine" energy. I'm happy to say that we're slowly moving away from that interpretation, instead viewing Venus as a symbol of connection and attraction, which of course has never had anything to do with gender in the first place.

Venus toggles between leading the sun and following behind it, which affects its appearance in the sky, and is never more than two zodiac signs from it. When it appears in the early-morning sky, it's considered a "morning star," meaning it rises with the sun and ushers in the day with vigor and an appetite for life and presents itself as indomitable and powerful. When it appears in the night sky, after or around sunset, it's considered an "evening star." Venus is more subdued in its expression in this position (but no less powerful) and has an air of seduction and romance. Once every eighteen months, Venus goes retrograde, where it completes its journey from evening to morning star. During this forty-day period, it disappears from the sky altogether and reemerges as a brilliant, blazing light on the eastern horizon.

All this to say: Even our planet of love and beauty needs a little cosmic nap once in a while, which means that your creativity does, too. Venus retrograde periods can be times of profound self-discovery if we allow ourselves to pause and sink beneath the surface to explore what lies deep within our hearts. It's only when we aren't visible to those around us that we can do the soulful work of figuring out how we connect to our art so that we can connect more powerfully with others.

Venus will always represent what we love and value, but when it comes to creativity, it also shows us how we connect to others' hearts through our work and how we attract attention and support for our projects. At its most powerful, Venus helps us to understand how and why we love what we love so we can share it with others. To access Venus's potent magic, a softening is required. Practicing gratitude for the creative bounty in our lives is one way to do this. Gratitude for our minds, our hands, art supplies, a laptop, and even our dreams softens our hearts and helps us tap into this frequency of love. Also, the conscious pursuit of pleasure, including working on pieces of art that just feel *good,* can remind us of the latent joy in the process.

MARS

If we know Venus as our "feminine" planet, then it's likely you've been introduced to Mars as the planet of masculinity. Again, this concept is slowly changing. What's traditionally known as "masculine" energy is actually just active energy—it pushes you and your projects forward, melts away fears and doubts, and breathes a bit of bravery into our cosmic DNA so we can do what we came here to do.

Mars represents our vitality and energy. It's also where we source our motivation and willpower. One aspect that our current understanding of astrology doesn't touch on enough is how and where we "get" the motivation to do the work. For such an active planet with big-boss energy, it's interesting that we talk about it in terms of what we're given, or allowed, to have when it comes to motivation and willpower. It's a passive way of looking at a planet that's all about action.

Let's rethink it in terms of the creative process. What is it, at its core, that motivates you to sit down at your work space, day in and day out? The details of this will look a little different for everyone based on their Mars sign, house, and any aspects it makes to other planets in their chart, but when it comes to creatives, the magic can usually be found in the vision. Whether it's a vision of how you plan to explore the inner depths of a character, or the dream of your painting hanging on a gallery wall, it's the promise of getting close enough to our inner glow that keeps us going. Only then can our sun light the match of Mars-driven motivation and send us on our way. And that's anything but a passive process.

The good news is that Mars only goes retrograde about once every two years, so we often have access to its powerful push in the direction of our dreams. And when it is retrograde, it's not that we can't continue moving forward, it's just that we may need to reassess what motivates us, finding different reasons to plug into our work when we feel tired and overwhelmed by the task at hand.

SPELLWORK: CREATE YOUR PLANETARY PLANNER

Let's recap what all these relatively quick-moving, personal planets mean to us when it comes to our creativity.

+ The sun: your highest inspiration
+ The moon: your body of work
+ Mercury: your message
+ Venus: your heart-to-heart connection
+ Mars: your motivation and the vision that fuels it

When you see them lined up like that, it becomes pretty apparent that the inner planets play a significant role in our day-to-day lives. It's possible that if we can get to know and work with all the aspects our personal planets represent, we can live a creative life that feels truly magical.

To create your personal planetary planner, take a look at each of these celestial bodies in your natal chart. Find the element and sign associated with each and write them down with this information in your notebook or grimoire. Then use the prompts below to begin to brainstorm how you can nourish and balance each of these planets as often as you can. Here's an example of how to do this with your sun sign.

My sun is in a [element] sign. [What the planet represents] is most accessible to me when I'm [insert activities associated with that element]. It's also in [zodiac sign]. I can nourish its place in my creative process through [insert activities associated with your zodiac sign]. Some ways I can do that in my day-to-day life are [brainstorm some practical things you can do to bring out the best of this planet].

Here's an example of what mine looks like for my sun:

My sun is in an air sign. My highest inspiration is most accessible to me when I'm playing with sparkly new ideas and communicating with others. It's also in Gemini. I can nourish its place in my creative process through invigorating conversation and socializing. Some ways I can do that in my day-to-day life are allotting time in my schedule to chat and brainstorm with like-minded friends and connecting with others.

From this point, I can begin to visualize how I can rework my daily rituals and routines to include more of what stimulates me emotionally, mentally, physically, and spiritually. Now go through each of your planets and fill in the blanks for their elements and zodiac signs. When you're finished, you'll be able to see how you can better work with the needs of each planet and maybe even how you haven't been giving parts of your creativity all that they need so you can tap into your special brand of magic.

THE OUTER PLANETS: YOUR MAGIC'S PLACE IN THE WORLD

It's one thing to want to create with magic for the sake of producing the things you've always dreamed of making. It's another to take it a step further and consider how your magic, and what you create with it, can impact the world.

When it comes to impact, it's easier to consider it in terms of ripples instead of splashes. Very few of us will create something of such magnitude that it will feel like a boulder being dropped into a lake, shaking up every last water droplet in an extremely profound way. And that's fine! Every single creation in this world still makes an impact, and most often, it will feel like a ripple. Sometimes, it will cause a single ripple inside your heart, forcing you to reckon with something you haven't been ready to face until now, until you could process it through your work. Other times, it will ripple outward, gently bumping up against the people who need it at that exact moment, whether it's twenty people or twenty thousand.

In modern astrology, the outer planets—including Jupiter, Saturn, Uranus, Neptune, Pluto, and the comet, Chiron—have a greater pull on how we, personally, fit into the collective as a whole. This is because these celestial bodies are coursing along a much wider ellipse, which means it takes them far longer to circulate through the zodiac. Because they are so slow-moving, they are more likely to impact a generation or microgeneration as a whole. That said, if one of these outer planets—especially Jupiter and Saturn—is making a strong aspect to your inner planets, you may feel the effect on a personal level.

JUPITER

The gas giant of our solar system is considered the first of two social, or transpersonal, planets. Both Jupiter and Saturn are the last two planets visible from Earth with the naked eye, yet they still take years to circle through all twelve zodiac signs. These two planets bridge the gap between the inner and outer planets, helping us to understand how our personal lives impact the times we're living in and the culture at large, and vice versa.

In Western astrology, Jupiter is a symbol of expansion. It's also known as the planet of luck and abundance, and it can denote where we're expected to show up in the world in a big way. When it comes to our creative lives, Jupiter represents where we'll find *the most opportunity for our work to make an impact*. This magnanimous planet shows us the way to recalibrating our personal lives and preferences to include others. It can help us understand that nothing we create is in a vacuum and that when we present it to the world from a place of truth, we can expand in ways we never thought possible while simultaneously adding new ideas to the collective culture.

It takes Jupiter about twelve to thirteen years to circle through the zodiac, which means that by the time it returns to the position it was when we were born (also called a *Jupiter return*), we've had many years to both earn and absorb its wisdom while growing in new and exciting ways. From here, we can attract even more opportunities that will stretch us in fresh and exciting ways.

Working with jovial Jupiter calls the magic-maker to tap into the meaning of joy. When we approach life as a continuous celebration of all that is and all that's possible, we tap into Jupiter's essence, thus opening us up to fresh ideas and exciting opportunities we may otherwise miss. Think of it this way: Wisdom and wonder are much easier to access when we're approaching our creativity as something to be revered. We begin to see mistakes and missteps as part of the process, experiences to honor instead of things to be ashamed of.

SATURN

The second of the transpersonal planets is our ringed beauty of many moons, Saturn. Where Jupiter expands all it touches, Saturn contracts. Perhaps you've already heard of something called a *Saturn return,* which is when Saturn returns to the position it was in at the time of your birth. The difference between this return and Jupiter's, though, is that it takes Saturn about thirty years to transit each zodiac sign, which means we only get two, maybe three, Saturn returns in our lives if we're lucky. These are considered monumental milestones and, to be honest, can really kick our asses. Because Saturn's job is to teach us about discipline and focus, Saturn returns can be a time of severe contraction where jobs, relationships, and projects fall away. Where a Jupiter return tends to bring in more, a Saturn return may be signified by loss, which is why this planet gets a bad rap.

The concept of a Saturn return has threaded its way into pop astrology. Frankly, it's just not as much fun as our fun uncle Jupiter. Instead, Saturn is the life coach of the cosmos, forcing us to drink green juice and get enough rest. We're better for it, and our work is better for it, but it's not as much fun as a Jupiter-fueled binger, let's be honest.

When Saturn is in a strong aspect to an inner planet or during your return period, it's time to grow up in whichever area of your life is being activated in your chart. Saturn requires us to grow into our maturity, and that's a good thing. An incredibly important thing. Without Saturn teaching us how to cut away any and everything that isn't for our best interest, we would never be able to get the kind of crystal-clear clarity required to create with authenticity and make an impact in the world.

The truth is, we can't do it all, as much as we'd like to. Saturn helps us to make grounded decisions around our projects, as well as what it takes to create from a place of soul-nourishing magic. If we're going to create something of meaning, whether it's just for our eyes or we plan to share it, we *will* be required to let go of other things in our lives and build stronger boundaries. Saturn's wisdom teaches us how to do so. To tap into all that Saturn has to offer, consider the steps to building any kind of structure. We start with the bare bones and create an outline, a frame, or skeleton. It's in this work of applying concrete form to both a project and your creative process that Saturn magic makes itself known. The work of routine, ritual, and boundary-tending is Saturn in action.

CHIRON

Discovered in 1977, Chiron has since been classified as an asteroid, minor planet, and comet. Unlike other celestial bodies in our solar system, it has an extremely erratic orbit, meaning it spends almost quadruple the amount of time in Pisces and Aries versus their opposite signs, Virgo and Libra. Chiron has been so tough to pin down that the first astronomer who plotted its path called it a "maverick." In astrology, Chiron is called *the wounded healer* and signifies our deepest wound that we're meant to transmute so we can serve others. If erratic ups and downs and the inability to categorize pain and grief isn't the perfect metaphor for healing, I don't know what is.

Chiron shows up between Saturn and Uranus—or between the transpersonal and generational planets (more on that in a second). If we're looking at its placement from a metaphorical angle, this denotes that while we may all have our wounds, there is also great meaning in understanding them and having compassion for ourselves. When we do the work of loving ourselves *because* of our pain, not only in spite of it, and showing ourselves this love even when we're at our worst, we unlock the gateway to our collective evolution.

Because let's be honest: As a society, we are never going to get anywhere while there are still so many deeply wounded people running around, talking and acting from a place of pain instead of love. Chiron encourages us to heal ourselves so we can help heal others. This process is extremely personal to each creative, and only through reflection can we begin this journey. Not only does the process of reflection allow us to mine our memories, relationships, and experiences for seeds we'd like to plant in our projects, but it can help us uncover the roots of our creative blocks, the fear of being seen through our work, and so many other heartaches we tend to bump against. Chiron work can involve traditional therapy, yoga, medication, a plant-based diet, deep rest, talking with friends, or any number of practices that help to soothe your nervous system so you can glean the wisdom it will require to heal your own wounds.

URANUS
Now we move from the transpersonal to the generational planets, which include our three outermost bodies: Uranus, Neptune, and Pluto. Because they take so long to transit through a single sign, the majority of a generation will have the same Uranus, Neptune, and Pluto signs. Translation: These planets impact us much more on a collective level, as in they're working to help shape us into the people we

need to be to play our part for the good of society. That said, when one of these powerful planets is activated—or transiting one of your personal planets, in your chart—change of all kinds is usually on the cosmic agenda.

When Uranus was discovered in 1781, it blew apart our understanding of the cosmos as we knew it. Until that point, scientists believed that our solar system ended with Saturn, but this electric-blue planet that rotates on its side hopped into our collective consciousness, reminding us that there is always something new and radical to discover. Historically, the discovery of Uranus fell right in line with the transition between the Enlightenment and the Industrial Revolution, which, as we know, changed the world forever.

Uranus is our planet of liberation. When it's active in your chart and making strong connections with any of your inner planets, you can be sure that a personal revolution is on the horizon. After the structure and discipline of Saturn, which asks us to grow up and use our gifts to further society, Uranus bursts onto the scene to shatter social norms. It makes sense, really. Of course we'll always try to fix things within the structures and systems we've already built, but at some point, it becomes apparent that the whole thing needs to be broken down and remade for our highest collective good.

Uranus can bring forth both the gain of Jupiter and loss of Saturn in terms of our creative process. It asks us to look at how our projects can cause a ripple in the collective, to change the hearts and minds of others, while also stripping away our safety nets so we can do this work. It's both the drive to expand your reach and the sometimes-necessary act of throwing it all in the trash and starting over again. This is how we access the wisdom of this unconventional planet—by adopting practices that move us toward liberation. If abiding by a strict schedule frees you from doubt and anxiety, move in that direction. If having more time to think, dream, and play enlivens you, then move toward that daily rhythm. Whichever frees you is the path to follow.

NEPTUNE

As we move farther away from Earth, the outer planets begin to have less of a personal impact and more of a collective one. A lot of that reasoning has to do with a planet's ecliptic, or orbital path. Neptune is so far away that it takes about 165 years to complete one lap around the sun, which means it's in each sign for about fourteen years. It's very likely that most of the people you grew up with have the same Neptune sign you do, as it impacts groups of people as a whole.

Neptune is the great boundary-dissolver. It's our planet of dreams (both literal and metaphorical), the subconscious, spirituality, and our imagination. If that sounds lovely, well, it is, but Neptune also rules the often-blurry line between perception and reality, which means it can stir up a bit of confusion. When Neptune is active in our charts, we can step through the veil and access a power beyond the physical to help inform our creativity. At the same time, we can be more susceptible to absorbing others' thoughts and feelings as our own since Neptune dissolves *all* our boundaries.

There is a lot of magic in working with Neptune as an artist. What is making art if not dissolving boundaries—between the seen and unseen, the heart and mind, you and me? Neptune in your chart can show you how your imagination expresses itself, as well as how you can activate it. One of my favorite practices for working with Neptune is sacred alchemy. It may sound intense, but alchemy is just the melding of two seemingly different substances. When I work with Neptune's magic, I often pull cards from different decks and mesh their meanings together, or pull lines from separate books and do the same. I'm consciously dissolving boundaries between insights and ideas so as to create something truly unique.

PLUTO

A planet, then not a planet, then . . . maybe a planet? While science can't quite decide where Pluto stands, astrology continues to hold fast to the concept of Pluto as a significant celestial body. One foundational idea behind astrology is that we continue to discover new pertinent planets as *we* evolve on both a scientific and soul level. Discovering Pluto and baptizing it as part of our solar system was never a mistake; we were able to see it when we were ready to do so. There's no turning back now.

Although when it comes to Pluto, we may prefer to look in the other direction. Pluto is our planet of transformation, and huge, soul-shifting change is really, really hard. Pluto requires *all* of us—our courage, mental fortitude, and whole damn heart—to make the kind of change that will be required of us on our life journey. And that's the thing: Transformation in at least one area of our lives *will* be required of us. We all have Pluto in our charts somewhere, and taking an inner journey through hell and back isn't for the faint of heart.

Luckily, this planet (I'm still going to call it a planet) also shows us how we can access our power. Like we discussed in part 1, power isn't a bad thing; it's incredibly important to claiming our future and making an impact. In our personal charts and creative process, Pluto shows us our own potential for transformation and how our work can be the trigger point to the transformation of others.

Working with Pluto is a precarious thing. On one hand, change is an inevitable part of life and creativity. Just when we think we've mastered our process, we are thrown for a loop and are forced to grow and evolve. On the other, invoking transformation before we're ready can cause us more harm than good. How many times have you been stuck on a creative project because something else in your life was going through a major transformation? I know it's happened to me multiple times, and I'd prefer if it didn't happen again, although the universe does what the universe wants.

Tapping into Pluto's magic is an act of attention and devotion. Its magic is unlocked by working with the planets that come before it. As we do this, we become masters at reading patterns and accessing our magic so that when the call to transform whispers to us, we'll know exactly how to ride the waves of change.

SPELLWORK: TO BE OF COSMIC SERVICE

Here's a recap of the meaning and metaphors behind the outer planets:

+ Jupiter: opportunities for expansion
+ Saturn: boundaries and maturity
+ Chiron: our deepest wound
+ Uranus: our liberation and the liberation of others
+ Neptune: highest imagination
+ Pluto: transformation

The message behind the outer planets isn't as clear-cut as the inner planets. They are less personal and gently nudge us to look at ourselves in a much broader light. With the inner planets, we asked ourselves, "How can we leverage this energy to create with more efficacy?" With the outer planets, we shift our focus to "How can we leverage our energy to create a whole new world?"

With this question in mind, go through each of these planets in your natal chart and write down which element and sign they were in when you were born. Then use the prompt below to help you start to piece together how your work can make a ripple in the world.

My Jupiter is in a [element] sign. I expand and attract opportunities when I [sign attributes and actions].

My Saturn is in a [element] sign. When I set boundaries around [sign attributes and actions] I can do my best work.

My Chiron is in a [element] sign. My wound may be related to [sign attributes and actions].

My Uranus is in a [element] sign. I liberate myself and others by [sign attributes and actions].

My Neptune is in a [element] sign. My imagination is whispering to me to create [sign attributes and actions].

My Pluto is in a [element] sign. My lesson in transformation is around [sign attributes and actions].

KEY #3: THE HOUSES

While the stars of the show in astrology are the planets, we've seen how knowing the elements and signs those planets are in can help us understand *how* they communicate with us and vice versa. Another component that helps us see which part of our lives these planets have a lot to say about is the houses.

The planets are individual parts of you.

The elements are the way those parts express themselves.

The signs are the nuances and preferences of that expression.

The houses are *where* those parts tend to speak loudest.

The 360-degree circle of your natal chart is segmented into twelve "pie slices." Each slice is 30 degrees, which means that a planet can be anywhere from 0 to 29 degrees (plus minutes, but I won't take you that far down the rabbit hole) within a house before it moves on to the next. If a planet is positioned within a couple of degrees of a line that separates houses, it's considered to be *on the cusp*. Each astrologer has their own viewpoint of what it means to have a planet on the cusp, and you'll often hear people say that they're on the cusp when it comes to their sun sign. You get to decide for yourself how you feel about it, but personally, I don't put a ton of stock into cusps. My opinion is that if you were meant to be a Leo instead of a Cancer, then your soul would have made it so and that's that.

Setting up the house system in your chart is where the nuance of astrology comes in. If you're new to astrology and just want to generate a chart and get to work, you can skip this explanation. For anyone who's curious about going deeper and those who want to consciously choose which system they use to interpret their chart, read on.

When you choose to make a free chart online, the software is most often creating it with a Placidus system. I won't bore you with the specifics, but basically, it's a time-based system that creates the cusps of your houses based on which degree of a sign is on the eastern horizon. The parameters of each are based on how much time a sign spends on the horizon, which means that some houses will appear larger than others, depending on how far north or south from the equator you live. It's considered the most popular system of drawing a chart, although that is changing.

Another popular option is the Whole Sign system. This system calculates which sign your rising sign, or ascendant, is and creates your entire first house, from zero to twenty-nine degrees and some change, in that sign. That means you'll only have one sign per house, and each house will be equal in size.

Placidus represents the perspective of what's happening in the sky from your exact location on Earth, which technically makes it more astronomically correct. Plus, it's messier—just like life, just like us. That said, Whole Sign is cleaner and simpler and is a great way to set up a chart for beginners. There's no judgment whichever route you take (and, honestly, some sites don't even give you the option to choose which system you prefer). All systems have their flaws; you just have to decide which ones you can live with. Pick your poison and go with it.

If you've already created your chart and you have no idea which house system you used for it, it's all good. As long as your chart displays the twelve pie slices within the circle, you have everything you need to explore this third key. If you want to go back to the site later and check which house system its software uses, go for it.

Each of the twelve slices represents a different dimension of your life—and, in my interpretation, your creativity. There are houses that are more physical in nature, like the houses of financial resources and your daily routines and work life, and others that are more esoteric, like the houses of healing and philosophy. By the time a planet circles through all twelve houses, that part of you has worked through your identity, resources, relationships, ancestry, vision, spirituality, and so much more, which is why planetary returns are such a momentous occasion. That part of you has completed a full journey and can now move into the next version of itself.

Let's take a look at each house, including its traditional meaning, some modern context, and the parts of the creative process each represents.

FIRST HOUSE

Traditionally, the first house represents how you present yourself to the world. This includes your physical body and appearance—the first impression you make to others. A modern interpretation also includes your identity outside of your physical body. It's who you are *outside* of all your relationships or who you are when you're alone with yourself at the end of the day. In the creative process, this is *inception*. It's the spark of new life or the underlying urge to explore some uncharted area of your mind or even your life. It's the understanding that something is *out there,* and in order to find it, you have to embrace your authentic identity.

SECOND HOUSE

This is the house of resources. Traditionally, it represented property and physical assets, like money and property. However, nowadays, we've expanded our understanding of resources. Sure, cash money can still apply here, but so can intangible resources that we work to cultivate over time— like patience, courage, and wisdom. This house is also the house of *experience.* To understand how to bring an idea into form, we have to have our own unique experience in the physical world from which to draw upon. Our senses and the physical integration of our lived experiences give us the framework to understand that idea that lights a fire within us.

THIRD HOUSE

This is the house of community and communication. It's where we first begin to sense the difference between you and me and learn to communicate our wants and needs to the people around us. It's also the place where our first original ideas begin to develop, usually as a result of expanding our minds and absorbing new information. In the creative journey, the third house is the house of *development.* This is where our minds begin to put the pieces of our experience into context to create something truly unique. It's the house that asks us to oscillate back and forth between thinking and expression, over and over again, until the idea becomes clearer.

FOURTH HOUSE

In a natural chart setup, the cusp of the fourth house denotes the lowest part of the circle. Metaphorically, it also represents the deepest, most private parts of ourselves. It's our innermost thoughts and experiences, the parts of ourselves we hold closest to the vest, and the foundation of our lives. This is the house that holds space for experiences with our family of origin, for better or worse, our ancestors, and our sense of what the word *home* means to us. In terms of creativity, this is the part of our journey where we lay our *foundation.* Now that we have a clear idea that we'd like to bring into form, we can start to lay the groundwork to make something special. This can look like setting boundaries and cultivating a sacred space to create, but it also means addressing your deepest emotions around the project. What is it within you that yearns to work on this project, at this time?

FIFTH HOUSE

If you already know a bit about Western astrology, you may have read that this is our house of children and creativity. Personally, I believe every single planet and house influences how we express ourselves creatively. If you have planets in this house, it doesn't necessarily mean it's easier for you to create and that your life will be full of children. At its core, this is the house of *expression*. When you think about it, that's exactly what both art and children are—an expression of yourself. They are both your creations living outside of your body. After you've laid the foundation for your idea, you can enter into this house of joy, pleasure, and self-expression. This is the heady honeymoon phase of an idea, where you are playing with the idea and enjoying the act of creation. For some, this may look like doodling, drawing maps, making aesthetic boards, and playing with characters and scenes that feel extra fun.

SIXTH HOUSE

Creating from a place of pleasure is a lovely place to begin your work, but in the long run, we all need some structure. If you only create when it feels fun or when you're inspired, chances are you'll never finish that piece, or it'll take a lifetime to do so. When we shift from fifth- to sixth-house focus, we move in the direction of service and duty. Traditionally, this house represents our health, daily work lives, and the routines that keep us on track to meet our goals.

While it may not seem as much fun to create from this space, as we grow and mature, we learn that there's a sacredness in committing to yourself and your art in this way. In the creative process, this is where we put in the work. This house represents the *routines* and rituals we put into place to make steady progress. Working with this house includes clearing space in your day-to-day life for your project, streamlining your routines, and honestly, just committing to our work and ourselves, day after day, until it's done.

SEVENTH HOUSE

The seventh house marks the beginning of the second half of the chart, or when we begin to consider the "other." This is our house of partnerships of all kinds—romantic, business, friendship, and even the people that don't like us that much. When it comes to our creativity, this is our house of *sharing.* Eventually, we all get to the point in a project when we feel we're ready to share some or all of it with a trusted partner. You may be a creative who wants to share pieces of your work as you go, or you may be like me, who prefers to wait until the project is finished. Either way, tapping into the love and trust of the seventh house can help us view our work from another's perspective, which is invaluable.

EIGHTH HOUSE

Easily the most confusing of the houses, there doesn't seem to be a theme to all that this house encompasses. Western astrology denotes that sex, intimacy, the esoteric and taboo, shared resources, other people's money, and transformation all fall in this house . . . which is *a lot*. When you look at these concepts as a whole, though, it makes sense. This is the house of *merging*—with another person, with your resources, and with the universe.

After you've shared your work with a partner or partners, it's time to take it to the next level. This is the part of the process that requires you to sink deeper, into your craft for sure, but also into your own subconscious. This house holds space for you to transform your project through revision and reworking, then rebirth it into the world. It takes guts to go this deep, which is why this house represents *personal power* in the creative process. Think of it this way: You are a creative alchemist, distilling your work down to its essential ingredients and then mixing and blending them together in a way that rebirths it, and both you and your work are more powerful for it. The lessons of this house aren't for the faint of heart. This is where I find the sacred tools in this book especially helpful; astrology, tarot, and other oracles help me to see the essence of the project and rework it to amplify its power.

NINTH HOUSE

This is the house of expansion in all its forms. The ninth house shows us what it'll take for us to stretch our minds and adopt a new perception of the world, including our place within it. That's why long-distance travel falls under this house, as it often shifts our view of the world, as well as higher education and adventures of all kinds.

Once we've examined ourselves and gotten intimate with our art, it's time to consider how we will expand out into the world. In the creative process, the ninth house rules our *influence*, and no, not when it comes to your social media channels. Everything you create has some influence on whomever consumes it. This is the house where you decide what you'd like that to be and how far you'll reach to expand your reach in the world. If you decide you'd like to take your project public, you can work with this house by researching different options to do so and then taking a leap of faith. Expansion into the unknown requires both wisdom and gumption, and you access the gifts of this house when applying both.

TENTH HOUSE

Positioned at the very top of the chart, the tenth house signifies who we are in public. This is the house of our highest worldly aspirations for ourselves. All those awards and accolades you dream of? They fall in this house, as well as your public reputation and highest career aspirations.

While accolades are lovely, they don't have a place in the creative process. Remember, your creativity is your source of power, and the process by which you access it is first and foremost about *you*. Awards and accolades come our way based on other people's opinions of our work, and while they feel good to receive, whether you get them or not is out of your control. In terms of creativity, the tenth house represents a *culmination*. What that looks and feels like will be personal to you and your goals for your project. Perhaps a culmination point for you is publishing your work in some way. Maybe it's hanging it in your home or putting it for sale in your Etsy shop or giving it as a gift. When you take the time to decide what your culmination point will be for this particular project, you will also know exactly when you've reached it.

ELEVENTH HOUSE

Just after the culmination point comes the eleventh house, or the house of long-term hopes and dreams. This is the house that asks us to think beyond the art we've just made to consider our social impact. Traditionally associated with friendship, social networks, and visualizing the future, when we shift into the realm of the eleventh house, it's time to step back and take a bird's-eye view of our creativity as a whole. How does this one piece fit into your entire body of work? What does it say about you personally, and us collectively?

In the creative process, this is our house of *disruption*. While we can't control exactly how our work will make an impact on others, we can still allow it to make an impact on us as creatives. The eleventh house asks us to consider how we've changed since we began working on this project in earnest and to allow that disruption to transform us. As you reflect on this house, consider: What is it about the world at large that infuriates you? This flicker within us is a righteous response to injustice. From this space, ask yourself: How does my project address this injustice? Maybe it addresses it directly, but most likely, you'll find subtle themes and nudges threaded through the piece, and others that consume your work will, too. From this place of pondering, we begin to unravel our place in the collective and how we can continue to speak truth to power to create ripples of change.

TWELFTH HOUSE

The twelfth house is associated with healing, endings, and spirituality. This is the last house on our cosmic journey, and it's within the sanctuary of this house that we do the work of healing old wounds and finding our place in the universe so we don't make the same mistakes on our next trip around the sun.

The twelfth house is the house of *integration* in the creative process. If you're someone who always likes to be actively producing something, you may be tempted to skip over the lessons that this house has to offer and start right back on the creative journey again with a new project. But this house is just as important as any of the others. This is where we distill all the lessons we've learned, stitch them into something meaningful, and cut away all the loose threads that no longer serve our creativity. Working with this house requires stillness so we can discern the wisdom we'll need on our next go-around. Meditation, dream journaling, and good ol' deep sleep are critical here.

A NOTE ABOUT ASPECTS

By now, you've spent some time looking over your natal chart, and you've probably noticed all of the different-colored lines zigzagging through the center of the circle. These are aspects, and they denote the relationships between the planets. There's so much information you can glean by taking a closer look at how each planet interacts with the others in your chart. Analyzing the aspects is the fourth key to unlocking astrology, but this is as far as I'll take you on that journey in this book.

In truth, there is so much nuance in the way planets communicate and interact with each other that the depth of that topic can only be covered through a more intimate medium. If you're interested in learning more about your natal aspects, consider a personalized reading from an astrologer you trust.

SPELLWORK: YOUR COSMIC CREATIVITY GUIDE

Take one last look at your natal chart. Find which house each of your planets is located in. You can tell when a planet is in a house because its glyph, or symbol, will fall in the "pie slice" of that house. Alternately, some online chart generators also offer a list of your planets, their signs, and sometimes their houses.

When there are several planets in a single house, it denotes a concentration of energy, or an area of life that is or will become a focus for you. And if there are no planets in a house, that only means that this particular area isn't a major focus or pain point for you right now.

Some questions to ask yourself as you explore your chart are:

Is this area of life or the creative process a pain point for me?

Is this part of the creative process generally easy or enjoyable for me?

Knowing which houses are "active" (or have planets in them), how can I leverage this information to help me create with less friction?

Knowing which houses are empty, how can I flow with the open space in my chart and allow those less chaotic areas to support me?

Putting It All Together

This is only the tip of the iceberg when it comes to using astrology as a sacred tool. There is so much information and insight to glean from your chart, no matter how many times you look at it. As you evolve as a creative, what you notice in your chart will also change and become more relevant to you. The point is to continue exploring, and to come back to your chart again and again, especially when you feel fragile or nervous or stuck. Remind yourself of the gifts the planets have for you, as well as what you can do within your power to leverage them. You can also look at your chart as a reminder of the parts you tend to have difficulty with, not to discourage you but so you can use your strengths to support yourself through the hard parts. That is how we keep growing, evolving, and making—by acknowledging our greatness while simultaneously humbling ourselves so we can be honest about the parts where we could use a little, or a lot, of help.

8

TAROT

MAYBE YOU'VE SEEN one of those movies where a character goes to a psychic reader. They usually have to walk through some kind of beaded curtain, then sit down at a small table in a dank room while a person wearing a lot of eye makeup sets out cards. From there, you see the reader set out cards with a flourish, and almost always the Death card comes up. There's usually some talk about literal death, how life is going to suck, on and on. It's all very dramatic.

And unrealistic.

I get that it's *supposed* to be dramatic for the show or movie, but if that's the only exposure you've had to tarot, you're definitely missing some important information about this sacred tool. And that's exactly what it is: a sacred tool that you can use to tap into your magic and highest creativity.

Like astrology uses the metaphor of the cosmos to help unearth new insights about yourself, tarot speaks through the lush imagery and classic interpretation of its cards. Both tools act as a portal to self-discovery and, in my opinion, are at their best when you use them to empower and illuminate your practice. Both tools help you to access your own magic in a real, tangible way. Some creatives prefer one over the other, while others (myself included) use a blend of both.

On that note, I think it's also important to discuss what tarot is *not*. Personally, I don't use it to predict the future whatsoever. Some modern mystics do, but please know that you can use tarot without any focus on prediction. It's also not a tool of the devil. It's not Satan speaking through the cards to get you to do evil. The cards don't carry curses. You aren't going to hell if you use them.

You get the point.

All sacred tools are neutral; they are neither good or bad. They are simply a way to see yourself, your life, and your creativity from a new angle. And the best part? You always get to decide for yourself which insights you'll hold on to and which you'll let go of for now. The power is in your hands, not the cards.

BREAKING DOWN THE DECK

A true tarot deck is a set of seventy-eight cards—no more, no less. There's a specific number of cards that appear in a specific order, and together, they tell the story of the querent (that's you). Originally used as playing cards in fifteenth-century Europe, their use eventually evolved as a divination tool in the eighteenth century. From there, three "brands" of tarot cards emerged, with the Rider-Waite deck and its illustrations the most common iteration you'll find in bookshops and occult stores today.

Among those Rider-Waite–based decks, you'll find hundreds, if not thousands, of different designs. There are decks with ghosts representing the characters, decks full of cute and cuddly cats, goddesses, Disney characters, plants, and more. These are all considered tarot decks as long as they have the standard seventy-eight cards.

Also on the shelves, you'll find tons of decks that don't have seventy-eight cards. They may have any number of cards, either more or less than a tarot deck, and they don't subscribe to the traditional card order. These are called *oracle* decks, which are a bit different from tarot. Because an oracle deck can be made of any number of cards, with any imagery, and a variety of interpretations, they fall under a different category of tools. We'll discuss them more in the "Other Oracles and Tools" chapter.

While the imagery may vary between tarot decks, the two sections the cards are divided into are always consistent. There's the Major Arcana, which is composed of the first twenty-two cards in the deck. These cards depict the querent's journey from beginning to end, and often represent higher soul-purpose matters of fate. The other fifty-six cards are a part of the Minor Arcana, which is separated into four suits. These cards represent the ups and downs of daily life and are usually interpreted as events that aren't set in stone.

THE MAJOR ARCANA

This "section" of your tarot deck represents all the different aspects of a world-shifting journey. Depending on the question you ask your cards, this journey can be literal, as in plans to move across the continent, or metaphorical, such as the journey of a relationship, career path, or self-discovery. As we've seen, the process of accessing your highest creativity is also a journey, and it can also be represented by these twenty-two lush and potent cards.

When a Major Arcana card comes up in a reading, it's a call to pause and reflect. These cards represent archetypal energy and spiritual lessons, and their meaning may not always be clear at first glance. These cards often relate to the broader themes of your life and the lessons you're learning or should be paying attention to right now, and honestly, it's not always easy to see the wider, sweeping cycles and themes of our lives when we're just trying to catch our breath. That's what makes the Major Arcana such a powerful tool—working directly with these twenty-two archetypes helps us to stand still long enough to see the greater meaning to our work and lives.

While each of these cards has their own traditional meaning according to the original Rider-Waite system, there's also room to interpret them as steps along our creative journey. Let's take a walk through each of the Major Arcana cards and their modern interpretations.

0: THE FOOL

Typically depicted as an androgynous person wearing a rucksack and stepping off a cliff, the Fool represents the ultimate leap of faith. And what is making art but a world-shifting leap into the unknown? It doesn't matter if you've done it a hundred times or this is your very first project, taking that first step off solid ground is always a little terrifying. You know that once you begin this journey, you will never be the same again. But remember, the Fool doesn't take the leap completely unprepared. They've brought their rucksack, and there's a dog by their side. Consider: What are the essential tools you need to pack with you on this journey? And who is your most trusted and loyal companion that can accompany you, at least in spirit?

1: The Magician

A powerful person stands before an altar, one hand pointing toward the sky and the other to the earth. It's quite a departure from the joyful innocence of the Fool. This card doesn't mean that you're already a master magician, but it encourages you to *think clearly about your next steps.* We always have to take the leap of faith first to open up space for the universe (and our imagination) to meet us halfway, but then we need to pause and collect ourselves before we continue. The leap is the moment you decide to commit to a particular project or process, and it's supposed to be at least a little scary so as to shake you awake. But to make the kind of art you've always wanted to make, you need focus. The Magician shows us that we have the power to become the alchemists of our destinies, but we have to be crystal clear about what we want and why we want it, then gather the tools and strategies we'll need to make our magic. These will vary from project to project. Some projects you may collect a ton of tools, including everything from new paints to software to oracle decks, crystals, and candles that are just for *this* work. Other projects may require less of you, only asking for your fullest attention and an open heart.

2: THE HIGH PRIESTESS

Where the Magician works to assemble all their tools so they can create magic, the next card in the journey, the High Priestess, represents *receptivity* to the mystical. They are the keeper of universal wisdom, the psychic, the intuitive, the space from which all ideas live, and most important, a crucial step to tuning in to what your magic is saying to you.

Before you can move forward on your creative journey, it's imperative to strengthen your connection to your own inner wisdom. Think about it: What's the point in collecting all the tools if you don't know how to use them in the most aligned, efficient way possible? In practice, this may look like meditation, daydreaming, and anything that allows your subconscious to work behind the scenes. You'll know you've hit upon something profound when you *experience a visceral reaction* to a thought that pops up. For some creatives, this is felt in the body through chills, tingling, or the flip-flop feeling you get in your stomach when riding a roller coaster. For others, it may be a swell of emotion that feels misplaced, or it may appear as a "random" thought that makes you wonder where it came from. Pay attention. There's wisdom in the whispers.

3: THE EMPRESS

The Empress card usually depicts a powerful, pregnant woman sitting upon a throne, surrounded by lush scenery and symbols of Venus, including the planet's glyph inside a heart. At this point in your creative journey, it's time to take the tools you've collected and combine them with the intuitive wisdom you've gleaned to create something new, exciting, and wholly *you*. The Empress represents the process of becoming a vessel for your highest creative aspirations. This is the first active part of the journey, where you are following your instinct and experimenting with your tools as you begin to create in earnest. To do this, you'll lay out all your tools and wisdom before you. How will you use these tools to bring these insights about your project to fruition on the page, canvas, or another medium? If you're feeling an urge to create a project around grief, for example, which of your tools can help you tap into that potent emotion so you can translate it into your work? This is also the point where you'll gather any other tools you may still need to help you on your journey.

4: The Emperor

Sitting proudly upon his throne, the Emperor is a call for stability. As the counterpart to the Empress, the Emperor helps us to put order to our work. His archetype may feel a little less fun than basking in the raw creative power of the Empress, but let's be honest: Structure and order are how we get the work done. At this point in the creative journey, you've begun to get a sense of what wants to be made through you. The Emperor asks you to now build structure around that energy, for both your creative process and the project itself. How will you order your days and structure your time to create so you're working most efficiently? And what do the "bones" of your project look like? It's time to put a frame around your idea in whichever way works for you, your process, and the project itself.

5: The Hierophant

The Hierophant card depicts a person adorned with religious symbolism presenting before their congregation. They represent a mentor or leader who teaches a specific set of rules or standards. It's often associated with a religious leader because of the emphasis on tradition and conformity. When it comes to making things, though, conforming to society's expectations is a surefire path to misery. Instead of thinking of the Hierophant as conformity of thought, consider that it has much to teach us about the sacredness of ritual. It's through ritual that we show ourselves just how committed we are to the work, and through ritual, we can perform our rite of passage from maker to magician. We all know that creativity can feel unpredictable, both in what we produce on a day-to-day basis and what the final product will look like. Ritual can help to create a sense of predictability in the process, order to the chaos. No matter which project I'm working on, my ritual usually involves meditation, candle lighting, and card pulling. Your ritual may be similar, something entirely different, or may change with each project. It doesn't matter; it just needs to be yours.

6: The Lovers

Discipline and commitment will get you far, but they won't take you over the finish line, at least not in a way that feels both satisfying to you and whomever consumes your finished piece. Art always bridges a gap, whether it's between you and another or parts of yourself. The Lovers is our first consideration of that "other." This card depicts two people entwined in some way to demonstrate a conscious love. It's the point in your process, even before you get to work in earnest, where you remind yourself that this commitment you're making to yourself and your project is an act of love.

I want to be clear that while many creatives will consciously choose to share their work, plenty of others make for themselves and don't plan on sharing, or even want to consider bringing in another's energy into their work. It doesn't matter where you land; the love is still in the commitment. When you fine-tune your perception to view this project as a choice you make in love, how does it change the way you look at the work ahead of you?

The key word of this card is *communion*. That means with another person or an audience at large, sure, but at this part of the process, it means communing with all the parts of yourself—memories, experiences, emotions, and so on—to create potent and authentic work. It means making a promise to yourself that everything you do in service of this project is *also* in service to yourself. No harmful habits that will wreck your body while you create. No incessant negative self-talk. Each day before you start, remind yourself that this is an act of love on all levels.

7: THE CHARIOT

With the combination of structure, ritual, and connection, you're well on your way to creating the art you've always wanted to make. The Chariot card signifies this rapid forward movement toward your goal. This is the part of the process where all the foundational work you've done, including listening to your magic, communing with parts of yourself, collecting the tools you'll need, and taking care of yourself begins to pay off. You're in sync with your creativity. This is the time to follow the road wherever it may take you and allow yourself to be delighted by the synchronicities that arise.

8: STRENGTH

After the quick, yet steady, pace of the Chariot, you're now approaching the end of your *first version* of this project. This is where many creatives think the journey ends, but in reality, there are twenty-two cards in the Major Arcana, and we are only at the ninth card. There's plenty more to go.

As you reach the home stretch of this first iteration of your project, doubts inevitably seep in. Personally, I think this is a pretty standard part of the creative journey. When you are reaching the end of a phase (in this case, the initial phase of translating your idea into a product), you then have to decide what is the next step of your work. Whether you choose to release it into the world or keep it to yourself, you are changed because of your time with yourself and your work. The prospect of facing this new version of you can be intimidating. Like the person taming the lion in the Strength card, this is when you tame your fears and doubts and finish the first iteration of your creation.

9: THE HERMIT

The Fool at the beginning of the journey has now become the Hermit. In the traditional imagery, an old wise man stands atop a mountain, holding a lantern, which represents the inner glow of wisdom. After finishing the first iteration of your project, it's time for a well-intentioned pause. You've

just about reached the halfway point in both the Major Arcana and the creative journey. Where have you grown so far
during this project? What wisdom will you integrate and
take with you as you continue onward?

10: THE WHEEL OF FORTUNE

In the Wheel of Fortune card, we see how our priorities can
and do shift when the time is right. This is easily the most
symbolic card in the entire deck, and there have been lengthy
discussions on what each of the symbols means, including
the Wheel itself at the center of the card. In this interpretation, the Wheel represents the turning point in the creative
journey, from creating in a vacuum to involving others in the
process. This is where you shift from creative to consumer
and begin to consider how your work could fit into the wider
public domain. Dream big here, magic-maker. Where would
you like to see your work in the world?

If you're making just for yourself, there's still work to be
done on this journey for you, too. While some creatives will
begin to expand outward here, the rest will shift inward. If art
is not being made to share with an audience, then the act of
creating for yourself will inevitably call you inward to witness
and transform something once hidden. We never quite know
what it is until we're deep in the process, but this is the point
where you make a choice. Which direction will the Wheel
turn?

11: JUSTICE

The figure in the Justice card holds a sword in their right
hand and the scales in the left, signifying the need for both

intuition and logic to make clear-cut decisions in your best interest. As you begin to look at your piece from a different perspective, Justice encourages you to examine it with an unbiased eye. This midpoint of the Major Arcana—and the creative process—encourages us to move fully into the realm we chose at the Wheel. What needs to be cut or transformed to make your work into its highest iteration? The truth is, none of us gets to skip the reworking and revising part of the process. There is a precarious balance between the internal, solitary process of creating from magic and then shaping it into a piece that is worthy of the energy you've put into it. Justice is the first step in molding your raw creative power into a piece that can be of service to yourself and, if you wish, the collective.

12: THE HANGED MAN

The traditional imagery of this card depicts a man hanging by one ankle from a tree. It represents a pause that's not always planned for, as denoted by the way the man has been tied up and "trapped" by someone or something else. When we're talking about the creative journey, though, we can look to the Hanged Man's predicament as a shift in perspective. He's literally hanging upside down, forcing him to see his work from a new perspective. It's time to gain new insight, whether through a critique partner, joining a class or workshop, or spending a moment away from your project so you can come back to it with fresh eyes. You'll know it's time to return when things that were once unknowable are suddenly visible to you, as the creative.

13: DEATH

Easily the most recognizable card in the Major Arcana, the Death card usually depicts some version of the Grim Reaper riding a horse. But contrary to what popular media may have to say about it, the Death card actually represents transformation of all kinds. Pulling this card or working with its archetypal energy doesn't mean that you're going to die—at least not in the physical sense. It's symbolic of releasing something that isn't in your best interest, allowing a part of you to die so that you can be wholly transformed. This card denotes the point in the process where you must remake your work. You've seen it from a new perspective while working with the Hanged Man card, and now it's time to take that wisdom and do the emotional, mental, and physical work of transforming your project. Similar to the work you did with the Chariot card, you are again sitting in your work space, applying your fresh insights and revising this work. You're staring down the fears, doubts, and negative self-talk that may have started to creep in. You are doing *the work*. One thing's for sure: Neither you nor your art will be the same on the other side.

14: TEMPERANCE

The Temperance card depicts an androgynous angel holding two cups as they blend the elements inside. This angel has one foot in the water and one on the earth, symbolizing the sacred art of mixing elements to create something with a higher purpose. This archetype is similar to the Magician, only the Magician is simply a human who is collecting magic-making tools for the first part of their journey. Temperance depicts a spiritual being who understands that they now have to blend these elements to consider the spiritual, or highest, purpose for both the creative and the creation. This is another point in the journey where many creatives stop, thinking the work is complete. They've done the revising, reworking, and rethinking. They've sorted through their thoughts and emotions, and done the physical labor of bringing their project to fruition. It seems as if there is nothing left to do.

Temperance calls us back into balance, but please know that the way you used to go about your daily life won't look exactly the same as before you started the journey. You've created cracks in your viewpoint on art, magic, and yourself while working with the Death card, and it's through these cracks the light gets in. Now is the time to bring your life back into balance after the rigors of transformation. That might look like cleaning off your desk, putting away your tools, and returning all those ignored texts. It could also look like saying goodbye to old habits, cutting off ties with someone you realized is toxic for your mental health, or deep, nourishing rest. Allow the light to spill in as you figure out who you are on the other side of this act of creation.

15: THE DEVIL

Second only to the Death card in infamy, the Devil is one of the most visually intimidating cards of the Major Arcana. It usually depicts a literal devil presiding over two people who are naked and chained to both him and each other. It's never pleasant to pull the Devil card in a reading, but just like all the cards on this journey, it serves us to pay close attention to its message. The Devil represents our personal weaknesses and temptations, or the parts of us that cause us to self-sabotage. When we are pushing ourselves and our art to the next level, it's inevitable that the darker, fear-based parts of ourselves will start to get loud. This can look like letting your creative routine go off the rails, forgetting to take your meds consistently, or self-isolating. The Devil reminds us to keep an eye out for these patterns as we're working through the process of becoming the newest version of ourselves so we can recognize them for what they are: old patterns that once kept us safe but we no longer need. By naming them for what they are, they lose their power over us.

16: THE TOWER

After the darkness of the Devil comes the Tower card, which also isn't that comfortable to look at, to be honest. There's a bolt of lightning striking down from the sky, setting the Tower aflame and bringing the structure, and the people inside it, down to its foundation. Traditionally, this card denotes a sense of chaotic upheaval—the kind you don't see coming and can't prepare for. The Tower card is also a symbol of liberation. Through the lightning bolt of powerful, otherworldly inspiration, you are now at the part in the creative journey where you liberate the vision for your work, thereby liberating yourself and those who consume it.

To liberate means to free from limitations, and while that can be a painful process, it doesn't have to be devastating. The lightning in this card represents your magic, fully empowered. You've been working with and listening to it this entire journey, and now it's strong enough to deliver a potent message: *Free yourself.*

Perhaps you started this journey telling yourself you were just going to "see what happens," but then you found that you actually *can* record an entire album, from start to finish. Your work with the Tower is to free yourself from this self-imposed limit. One of my favorite ways to do this is to write down the belief I'd like to let go of, light the paper on fire, and bury the ash in my garden. Any way you choose, your own magic demands a reclamation. This way, when you start on the journey again, you continue to get closer and closer to art that is authentically you.

Tower energy could also call us to free ourselves of the work we've just completed. Now it's time to send the project into the world, whether that's through submitting it to a contest or sending it to your best friend. You are no longer bound by the thing you made, although there's still a bit further to go on the journey.

17: THE STAR

The Star card offers a much-needed reprieve after the intensity of the Devil and the Tower. In this card, a person kneels before a river with one foot in the water and the other on solid ground. After all that has happened on this journey, everything that isn't of consequence has been stripped away. All that's left is you and your magic. The Star card symbolizes renewal and recommitment. The Star shows us that there was always a reason for it all and that your power and creativity are even stronger for having embarked on this journey.

The Star calls us to a sense of awe and reverence. While

we are much wiser now, we are also still incredibly naive. And at this phase, we are probably starting to realize all that we still don't know about ourselves, our creativity, and magic in general. We can be proud of ourselves—absolutely. But we must also humble ourselves here. It's from this place of humility that our hearts and minds open once again, and the seeds of our next idea are planted into our subconscious in the fertile soil we've created. There's no definitive action to take, other than reflecting in gratitude for all that you've done and all that's yet to come. Reverence acts as a portal for magic.

18: THE MOON

Like the moon in astrology, the Moon card in the Major Arcana has a bit of an outdated interpretation. It's often associated with our subconscious fears and illusions, but personally, I think that's because the moon has long been a symbol of the feminine, and it's been gravely misunderstood. In its truest form, the Moon card represents our inner resources. What are the inner resources you've cultivated since you've started this journey? Perhaps you're kinder to yourself as an artist, or more patient, or you've learned that you can do hard things. Reflect on the resources you've gained so you can add them to your rucksack before you take off on your next adventure. You may even receive an intuitive nudge about which inner resources you'll need to leverage for the *next* idea that's already beginning to germinate in your subconscious.

19: THE SUN

Once we've collected our inner resources, we also need to consider our outer resources and supports. The sunflowers, bright light, and cheery vibes of the Sun card encourage us to reach out to the great, wide world around us to gather all that we'll need the next time we take the journey. Which supports do you now know you'll need when you start your next project? Again, you may already have an intuitive sense of the types of tools and strategies you'll need to cultivate before you head off on your next journey.

The Sun also represents warmth and celebration, so be sure to take a pause and enjoy your success at this point. *You* did that! This card serves as a reminder that while we can reflect and prepare for the next big thing, we also need to close this cycle, this circle through the Major Arcana, so as not to dilute our attention and energy by leaving a project open.

20: JUDGMENT

In the Judgment card, we see a person standing before an impressive angel, being judged for how they navigated their path. In truth, though, the only judgment that matters is yours. This is a time to consider how you will do things differently the next time around. The Judgment card is a symbol of rebirth, and it asks us to do the work to ensure that the next version of ourselves, and our art, is even closer to our magic.

This is the time to have a conversation with Future You, the one who has already started their next journey with a new creative project. What does that version of you want Present You to know before you begin again? You can journal or meditate on this concept and see what comes up. Another option is to write down everything you'll take with you in the next journey on one page, and everything you'll leave behind on another page.

21: THE WORLD

Finally, we come to the last card in the Major Arcana: the World. This is the card of completion and integration. After liberating your project into the world with the Tower, you've taken the time to consider the lessons you've learned and gather the inner and outer resources you need to replenish yourself and get ready for the next project. You've sorted through information and intuition with the Judgment card, and you probably already have a good idea of what to pack in your rucksack for your next big journey. But, for now, we close the circle.

The World card is another pause, this time to fully release everything we won't be carrying into our next loop around the Major Arcana. It's time to rest, recharge, and let go of the art you've created. Say goodbye to it. No matter who has consumed it, the acts of creation, transformation, and becoming even more of yourself belong to the World.

• •

SPELLWORK: YOUR MAJOR ARCANA ARCHETYPE

Now that you've been introduced to the cards of the Major Arcana, it's time to choose the card that you most identify with *right now*. Think about where you are on your creative journey at this moment. Are you just getting ready to jump off that cliff with the Fool? Or are you in a deep period of reflection and renewal after you've finished, like the Star?

Spend some time choosing which card represents you at this moment. If you have your own tarot deck, pull out that card and set it on your notebook or in your lap. If you don't have your own deck, pull up an image of the card from the internet (just type in the name of the card and then "tarot" in the search bar). Spend a moment gazing closely at the imagery, allowing your thoughts to wander a bit. What does the imagery remind you of? Is there a memory, feeling, or idea that comes up while you're spending time with this card?

Jot down any thoughts that arise while you're engaged with this card. Part of the magic of tarot is that the imagery on the cards can help us unlock our subconscious so we can hear the hidden messages we need to hear to create with more power. Write down everything that comes up, even if it doesn't make sense right now. Trust that it will as you go through this process.

• •

THE MINOR ARCANA

The other fifty-six cards in every tarot deck make up the Minor Arcana. Whereas the Major Arcana gives you a bird's-eye view of a situation, the Minor Arcana gets up close and personal with the day-to-day intricacies of life.

Some tarot readers consider the Major Arcana cards to be fated—themes or events that were always meant to happen to you at this point in your life. Minor Arcana cards, on the other hand, are occurrences that are subject to change. For example, if you ask your cards, "What do I need to know about my job today?" and you pull the Four of Swords, it could mean that your mind and body are calling for you to take it slow and easy at work. But maybe you decide to go back to bed to catch a few extra minutes of sleep and then fuel up on a healthy breakfast so you feel pretty good by the time you clock in, and you don't need to take it slow. The point is: The cards act as a mirror to your subconscious, imagination, and the universe for *exactly where you are when you're working with them*. When you pulled that Four of Swords, your energy was giving off the vibe that you needed rest. However, *you* changed that by giving your body some extra support before you started your day.

This is the nature of the Minor Arcana in a nutshell. The messages that these cards deliver are more malleable, and that's a good thing. Whereas working with the Major Arcana can feel a bit like watching a train barreling down the tracks and you have nowhere to go, the Minor Arcana gives us the sense of personal autonomy. Whatever is happening right now can change, and you can change the outcome by altering your perspective.

Because the Minor Arcana has so much to do with everyday life, and just by statistics alone, you're more likely to pull one as opposed to a Major Arcana card, their meanings tend to be much more personal. You see their imagery much more often and begin to relate it back to the events of your day or particular nuances of your creative process, and those cards start to take on a slightly different meaning from what's in the guidebook. For example, the Five of Pentacles typically represents financial hardships, but I've spent so much time with this card over the years that it's come to mean that I have all the creative resources I need right in front of me; I'm just not looking in the right direction. That personal meaning came from years of practicing with my deck and getting to know myself as a card reader.

The same will happen for you as you spend more time with your tarot cards. For that reason, I haven't included a card-by-card analysis of the Minor Arcana in this book. Instead, we'll consider the patterns and suits of the cards, as well as a closer look at the sixteen court cards. In the following section, we'll discuss how to develop your own meanings for each card and how to assess them in your creative journey as you become more and more familiar with them.

Remember: The guidebook that comes with your deck is just someone else's interpretation. It may be based on traditional language or imagery from the eighteenth century, but the way the author describes them is wholly their own. And if someone else can put meaning to the cards, why can't you do that for yourself, according to your own intuition and lived experience?

You can. I promise.

THE SUITS

In the traditional Minor Arcana, you'll find four suits: cups, swords, wands (also called *staves*), and pentacles (also called *coins*). If you're working with a more modern deck, you may find that your suits have different names. For example, *The*

Herbcrafter's Tarot divides the suits into water, earth, air, and fire.

Which brings me to my next point: The elements show up in tarot just as much as they do in astrology and nature magic. The good news is that you already have some familiarity with them, which should help you gain a deeper understanding of what each suit represents in the deck.

Cups

The cups are the suit that represent water energy. They denote a "feminine," or receptive, quality, which just means that they portray more internal experiences that can't always be defined by external stimuli or observable action. These cards represent our emotions and intuition—the deeper mysteries of our psyche. Oftentimes, guidebooks will also associate this suit with relationships, too, but if you think about it, it's through our connection with others that we can discern how we feel about someone or something. Cups cards in a reading ask you to examine your emotional undercurrent for the answers to your questions. In the creative process, cups insinuate that the answer we seek is emotional in nature. If we look closer at the way we feel about something, whether it's frustration toward a project or guilt for spending so much time on our art, we'll uncover the wisdom we need to move forward.

Swords

Words can cut deep, and the suit of swords shows us just how much damage they can inflict. Swords represent air energy. On top of the words we speak to others, they also represent the ones we think to ourselves when we're alone.

Unlike the emotionally fluid waters of the cups, though, swords call for precision—logic rules in this suit. You'll find a variation on what this means as you journey through these cards. There are cards representing logic when making an important choice, cards asking the querent to rest the mind, and even cards that represent haunting nightmares and mental anguish. When swords come up in your reading, there's a call to think carefully through a problem and to rely on evidence and logic to conclude. In the creative journey, swords remind us that there's a place for logic within the mystical realm of magic. These cards call you to cut through the fog and think critically about your work, whether that looks like choosing the next project based on which could be a commercial success or a callout letting you know your mind is in no shape to be making important decisions right now.

WANDS (STAVES)

The suit of wands, or staves, is willful, passionate, and highly inspired. It's more "masculine" in nature, meaning its imagery and messages denote a more active approach to a given situation. There's a sense of adventure in the wands, coaxing us out of our comfort zone and into a more expansive world. Traditionally, this suit represents creativity as a whole, but as discussed in the chapter on elements, the wands are truly about following through on inspiration. Any journey that will transform you, whether that's travel, an athletic challenge, or a creative project, can fall under the realm of this suit. When wands show up in a reading, you're called to trust your instinct and use your willpower to take a leap of faith. When working with your creativity, wands cards encourage you to just go for it. Go on; explore that nudge. Move with quickness. You're more than ready to act, so don't be afraid to dive all the way in on that project of your heart.

PENTACLES (COINS)

Pentacles, or coins, represent earth energy in the deck. These are the cards of physical substance, groundedness, and doing what needs to be done to accomplish our work. While they're often associated with career and money, it's important to look at this suit from a broader perspective to truly understand it. Your money and how you make it are essential to your physical well-being in this world—that's just how it is. But at their core, pentacles are asking us to consider worth as a concept. What we value will shine through in how we create the form and structure of our lives, how we spend our time, and yep, how we make money, too. Being so rooted in the physical, the suit of pentacles asks us to tap into our five senses and the structures we build to find the answers we seek. This is also true for their relevance in the creative journey. Pentacles show us how to lay a firm foundation and build up from there. Their wisdom shows us how to look for new opportunities and resources, set up a routine and structure that works for us, and work steadfastly toward our goals.

ACES THROUGH TENS

Each of the four suits has ten numbered cards (in this instance, the ace represents the number one, or the first card in the suit). Each of the numbers has an overarching meaning behind it and represents a part of the journey. Once you learn the basics of the numbers and the suits, it becomes much easier to re-member what each individual card means, too.

ACES
A spark of initiation or a new idea. These cards usually rep-resent a catalyst related to their suit that begins the jour-ney. The Ace of Swords represents a thought or stream of thoughts, whereas the Ace of Pentacles could represent fi-nancial resources needed to gather your materials for a new project.

TWOS
Balance and partnership. These cards denote the forces that will drive your decision—of which you'll face many on the creative journey—whether that's love, like in the Two of Cups, or logic, like in the Two of Swords.

THREES
Community and crossing the threshold. The threes are ac-tive cards that depict a point of no return, although in vastly different ways according to their suit. The Three of Cups depicts a celebration point in the journey, while the Three of Swords depicts wisdom gained through grief that can be translated into art.

FOURS
Stability and structure. These cards denote a pause to con-sider which tools and supports you need to call on as you create. The Four of Pentacles shows us someone who is holding on tightly to their physical resources, like money,

while the Four of Swords depicts a knight pausing to rest and recharge.

FIVES

Change and upheaval. Good thing you took a moment to build a solid foundation, because when the fives come around, a little chaos follows. This is your opportunity to learn from the chaos and apply the order you know you need to continue forward on your magic-making journey. The Five of Wands depicts an all-out brawl, which can represent a fight with others or ideas competing for your attention. Ask yourself: *What needs to change so I can continue on this path?*

SIXES

Cooperation and harmony. The sixes begin the second half of this journey and, after the conflict of the fives, encourage us to embrace peace in all its forms. While the Six of Wands depicts a victorious, celebratory scene, the Six of Swords shows us that we know it's time to move on because we deserve better. There's a sense of peace in both, although one is more bitter-sweet than the other. When a six shows up in a reading related to your creativity, the answer to your question lies in which-ever direction will lead you to greater harmony.

SEVENS

Wisdom and faith. At this point in the Minor Arcana, it's time to take a moment to think and act from a higher plane. These cards depict tricky situations you may be faced with, but also assurance that you have the inner resources to figure them out. The Seven of Swords warns against rash thinking and moving ahead without considering all lines of thought, while the Seven of Cups warns against giving into immediate temptation when faith is called for. In the creative journey, pulling a seven calls for the same level of discernment. Think about what got you to this point, and pause to look at the situation from a higher plane. There's a way forward if you're willing to expand outside your comfort zone.

EIGHTS

Dedication and aligned action. The eights ask us to recommit—not necessarily to the path we started on at the ace but to the new version of ourselves that has blossomed along this journey. In the Eight of Cups, we see a person leaving behind a stack of cups that used to be fulfilling, but is no longer. The Eight of Pentacles depicts a craftsperson toiling away, nose to the grindstone, thereby showing us that even the most rewarding pursuits still require hard work. As we know, we will inevitably change and grow on our creative journey; the eights of all suits show us what that recommitment to ourselves and our art looks like.

NINES

Deeper meaning and the cosmic ripple effect. We've almost reached the end of the Minor Arcana by the time we get to the nines. At the brink of completion, we're poised to consider the higher purpose of this journey and how our actions have caused a reverberance in the world. On one hand, we have the Nine of Cups, which signifies complete emotional satisfaction with all that has transpired. On the other, we have the Nine of Swords, which depicts someone wrought with spiraling thoughts over how things could have been different. When nines come into play, we're called to look at our project and process from a wider angle. Are we satisfied with the cosmic ripple we've activated? Has this process worn on us, and how can we mitigate our worries?

TENS

Completion and integration. The tens are the highest expression of the suit and the culmination of our journey from the ace. The Ten of Cups and Ten of Pentacles depict pleasant endings full of joy and prosperity. The Ten of Wands depicts a heavy load to carry across the finish line, with the hope that the querent will take this lesson into consideration before they begin the next journey. The Ten of Swords shows us that eventually both words and thoughts catch up to us in the end, so be sure to choose them wisely. No matter where you are on your creative journey, when you pull a ten card, there is a moment of integration afoot. You are called to pause and consider this sacred point. There is wisdom you've learned thus far that wants to be used as you go on. How can you integrate it into your project and process for the rest of the way?

THE COURT CARDS

Finally, we have the sixteen cards that make up the court cards. While most readers are pretty much in agreement as to the general meaning of a card or suit, we haven't come to a consensus on how to interpret these people-centric cards. Some readers say that these cards—made up of pages, knights, queens, and kings of each suit—represent actual people in our lives. Some say they're personality traits, maturity levels, or even events.

Personally, I read the court cards as aspects of ourselves. My belief is that tarot is a tool that helps us unlock our own magic, and that starts and ends with us. Court cards have a special place in the creative journey, and I find that I often pull them when I need to have a long-overdue conversation with part of myself. For example, when I was recently stuck on a project, I asked myself what I needed to know that I couldn't see. In came the Knight of Wands. As we've explored in this chapter, wands represent fast-moving fire energy, and the knight is a card of forward movement. This card was a call to converse with the most courageous version of me—the version that burns with inspiration and isn't afraid to pursue it. After some reflection, I realized that I had been stifling my magic and creating with caution when, truly, I'm a creative who prefers the intensity of burning things to the ground. From that point on, I moved with greater ease through the project.

All this to say, both reading your cards and embarking on the creative journey are deeply personal experiences, and no other person's opinions, ideas, and even presence matter as much as your own. Truth be told, when you are focused and committed to working with your magic, the influence of other people tends to wane, anyway. They are still important, and you can still love them fiercely, but their opinions or actions have no bearing on your path of self-discovery.

When a court card comes up in a reading, I first consider its suit. If it's wands, I think of the card in terms of action and passion. For cups, I read through the lens of emotion and intuition. Swords are logical thought, and pentacles are earthly resources.

Then, I consider where the card falls in the hierarchy. Pages are depicted as children and represent the lowest station. Then there are knights, who are teenagers, queens who are the second-in-command adults, and kings, who are the rulers. In my interpretation, pages are considered immature, or just beginning to understand their passions, emotions, thought patterns, and resources. This is typically a call to converse with a past version of myself, whether it's me as a child or the version of me who was once a beginner. There's wisdom to be found everywhere, even within our innocence, before we knew better. Working with the energy of the pages can help you to see a problem with a lightheartedness and purity while reminding us that we don't have to be martyrs for our work; we are allowed to create from a place of joy.

Knights represent rapid forward movement but can often be reckless. At their core, the knights act in service to the royals and are a metaphor for practical steps that push you to your highest good. Pulling a knight is a call to act. Just text your aunt and ask if you can borrow her drum set. Start the cross-stitch. Buy the paints. Get moving.

Queens, just like kings, represent mastery over their suit's focus, but in a different way. Queens are more receptive in that they understand the wisdom on a deeper level and can apply it to their own lives with ease. Queens tend to come up in my readings related to creativity and magic when I need a reminder that *I already know the answer.* Queens call us to converse with the wise person inside us, because they already know exactly what we need to continue onward.

Kings take that mastery a step further and apply that wisdom to the collective. King cards ask us to lead in whichever way we're called to do so. In the creative journey, they encourage us to unapologetically shine while still acting in the best interest of others. They ask us to consider (or reconsider) how our wisdom, magic, and creativity can positively impact the world.

Again, this is my personal practice based on how I teach and use tarot. As you get to know your cards and yourself, you may find that this method of interpretation isn't for you. At the end of the day, the tools you're using have to serve and empower you, or else they've gotta go.

- -

SPELLWORK: GET TO KNOW YOUR DECK

The easiest way to learn tarot is to work with your deck in a way that makes sense to you. It definitely helps to understand the elements, suits, and numerology of the cards to give you some hints, but making a personal connection to the card's imagery is an extremely effective method to store that information in your long-term memory.

Shuffle your deck until you feel ready to stop. Then choose one to three cards. Flip them over, one by one, and spend a moment gazing at the imagery. Take in all the details. Is there an experience, emotion, or memory that comes to mind while you're interacting with this card? If you're having trouble coming up with something, go back to the earlier sections in this chapter. Remember: Identify the suit the card belongs to first. Then look at the key words for its number. Once you have a structure for its meaning, it may feel easier to fill in the details with your own personal connections.

Make sure to jot down your insights as you work with these cards. If you're a beginner, you may even decide to do this activity with a card or two per day as you get to know them better.

TIPS FOR READING THE CARDS

We'll go over some specific methods for using the cards to amplify your creative magic in part 3 of this book, but for now, let's talk about general tips to follow when you're reading so you can feel confident in your interpretation.

First, you want to be sure you have a little talk with your deck before you get started. As we know, the most efficient tools give us some structure while still allowing them and us to evolve. The meanings you've assigned to your cards now may not always stay the same as you grow in your practice. Because there's some fluidity here, you want to be clear right from the onset what these cards mean in *this* reading. If you want your court cards to represent actual people for a particular reading, then state that out loud as you're shuffling them so that your subconscious gets the message, too. If you randomly decide that you want all cups cards to represent a piece of art you're making or a certain relationship or anything else, then go ahead and declare it.

Another part of being clear from the onset is assigning a particular placement for each card. When you pull more than one tarot card at a time, you're automatically creating a spread. There are spreads that are only two cards and others that use the entire deck. In my opinion, the most potent spreads are the ones that use only the exact number of cards needed to convey information without convoluting it. Each placement in a spread should represent the answer to a prompt or question. So, for example, let's say you want to use your cards to find out how you *really* feel about something you're trying to make. You'll need to decide what your cards mean to you beforehand, as well as what the placements mean. Maybe you decide on a simple one-card draw that answers the question, "How do I feel about this work?" Or maybe you pull two cards that answer questions like "What's blocking me that I can't see?" or "How can I get past this block?" The fun part is that you get to decide.

Another important part of reading is learning the language of your own personal magic. To do that, you have to embrace the idea that you just aren't going to know it all before you begin, and that doesn't mean that you can't take your best shot at an interpretation. Remember the Fool at the beginning of our journey, about to step off a cliff with nothing but a smile and rucksack? That's *you*, right now, on this tarot journey. So instead of running straight to the guidebook as soon as you pull a card, just *breathe* for a second. Absorb the imagery on the card. Let yourself swim in the intricate details, to wonder, to be curious, to assign your own meaning. And if you're practicing on someone else, take a leap of faith! Allow what you know about the basics to add form to your intuitive nudges and go for it. The worst that'll happen is that the reading won't resonate, which is totally fine. You can always try again.

After teaching tarot to a wide variety of students, both brand-new beginners and seasoned readers, I can say with confidence that everyone is much better at this than they think they are. I encourage people to try to read the cards without the guidebook at first, and they're pleasantly surprised at how close they are to the intended interpretation, anyway. Don't hold yourself back, and let your magic do the talking. You can't go wrong.

A Note About Reversals

In just about any tarot guidebook, you'll find an interpretation for a card when it's upright and a separate interpretation for when it's upside down. Reversals can happen for multiple reasons, and usually it has to do with the way you shuffle and sort your cards between readings. When you pull a card and it comes out upside down, you can choose to interpret it in a different way.

Like the court cards, there isn't a general consensus on how to interpret reversals. If you look on the internet, you'll come across a million different ways to read these cards. Some interpretations state that reversals hold the opposite meaning of their upright version. Others say that a reversal has the same essence as its upright version, only it's latent and will take some time to come to fruition. More interpretations see reversals as internal consequences instead of external stimuli, the lesson of the card coming to completion, and resistance to the card's message. Again, there's no wrong way to do this! You get to decide how you'd like to interpret the language of your deck, and that means adopting any of these reversal "rules" or making up your own.

If this all sounds like too much, there's another completely acceptable option: Don't read reversals at all. Even though I'm experienced with tarot, I very rarely read reversals, and only when I've set the intention for what they mean in *this* reading, in *this* spread, beforehand. Most of the time, if I pull a reversed card, I simply turn it upright and read it as is.

I do this for a couple of reasons. First, I tend to overanalyze the cards when I read reversals. And remember: When a tool doesn't empower you or help you see clearly, something has to change. I choose to keep tarot as part of my magic tool arsenal, but take out the reversals. Second, my tarot philosophy is that upright cards are capable of giving you all the information you need as long as you *ask the right questions.* The clarity of your questions greatly impacts the quality of the answers you get from the cards, and honestly, if you are precise in what you ask, upright cards can still tell you important information like if you're nearly finished learning a card's lesson, if you have internal resistance to a natural part of the creative process, and more.

ASKING THE RIGHT QUESTIONS

In all types of magic work, the intention you set is equally important as the actual application of your tools and strategies. In tarot, the questions you ask represent the intention you set for the reading.

If you ask a vague question like "What do I need to know about the book I'm writing?" then you can expect an equally vague answer. For example, let's say you asked that question and then pulled the Three of Swords, which depicts a bleeding heart pierced with three swords. You could interpret that any number of ways. It could mean that writing this book will require you to tap into hard-earned wisdom, or that it will break readers' hearts, or that your main character needs to go through a heartbreak, or even that writing it will cause you some anguish.

Instead, it's important to spend a little time carefully crafting your question. Not only is it good practice in magic work, it's also good practice for creativity in general. To really make an impact with your art, you have to be crystal clear with the message you're trying to convey. Crafting tarot questions is one way to practice precision and clarity.

All that to say, there's also a fine line between *too* precise and just enough. If you ask an extremely specific question, not only are you cutting off other possibilities, you're also hemming in both the cards and your intuition so they can't fully express their message. Questions that start with *when* and *where* tend to be too specific. For example, asking a question like "When will I publish my book?" is tricky because tarot isn't really set up to give you specific time frames. You could pull a card and look at the imagery for clues to which season that could happen in, but then again, are we talking about this year? Next year? A decade from now? Similarly, *where* questions may give clues in the imagery, but nailing down specifics is hard.

In the same vein, yes-or-no questions also usually don't work well with tarot. You could ask "Will I have my own gallery opening?" and pull the Eight of Pentacles. Well, the eight denotes hard work and dedication to your craft, so you could read that as a yes, you will have your own gallery opening in due time. You could also read it as you still have some work to do to hone your craft first. Besides, if the answer really is no, how is that serving you? You may feel disheartened and discouraged, and in that case the tool is not living up to its intended purpose.

Questions that do work well usually start with *what* and *why.* They offer a specific structure to your inquiry, while still giving your intuition a little wiggle room. Here are some of my favorite ways to start a tarot question:

+ *What do I need to know about . . . ?*
+ *Why is this lesson important to . . . ?*
+ *What is the next action I can take for . . . ?*
+ *What do I need to know about this situation that I can't currently see?*
+ *Why am I experiencing _____ at this time?*

TAROT SPREADS TO TRY

If the thought of making up your own questions and spreads seems intimidating, I get it, and I've got you. Here are a few tarot spreads I've made and used in classes, with clients, and for myself. Feel free to use any or all of these spreads as you work your tarot magic.

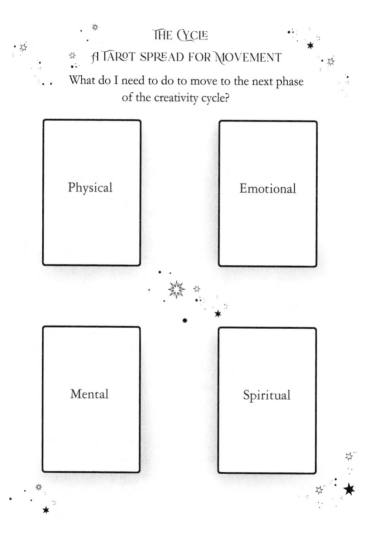

THE CYCLE

A TAROT SPREAD FOR MOVEMENT

What do I need to do to move to the next phase
of the creativity cycle?

Physical

Emotional

Mental

Spiritual

THE PRISM

A TAROT SPREAD FOR CLARITY

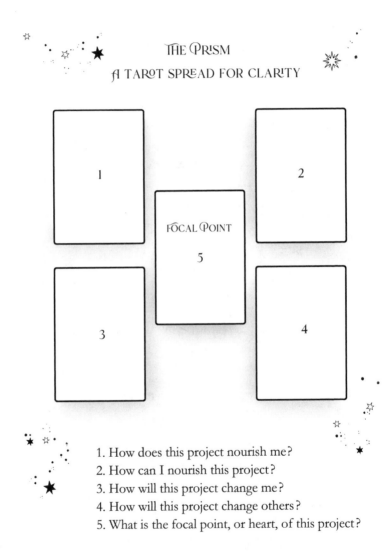

1. How does this project nourish me?
2. How can I nourish this project?
3. How will this project change me?
4. How will this project change others?
5. What is the focal point, or heart, of this project?

THE RELEASE

A TAROT SPREAD FOR BREAKING FREE

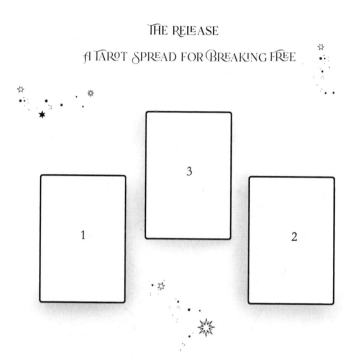

1. What is holding me back that I currently can't see?
2. What do I need to know to break past my limited beliefs?
3. What is waiting on the other side of this limiting belief?

THE PINKY PROMISE

A TAROT SPREAD FOR COMMITMENT

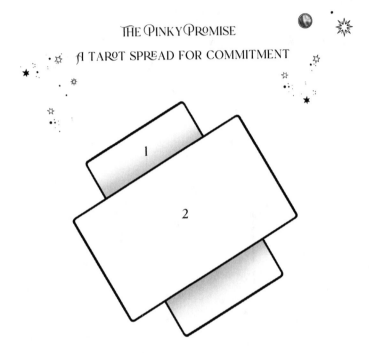

1. What is the promise I am fulfilling with this creative project?
2. How can I keep this promise?

9

OTHER ORACLES
AND TOOLS

~≼⫯≽~

WHILE ASTROLOGY AND tarot are two of my favorite tools to work with, there are so many unique and insightful tools out there to choose from. And you can even create your own oracles, too.

When we're talking about an oracle as a concept, its definition is a *divine message*. To me, a "divine message" is an insight that has a different tone and texture from your usual run-of-the-mill thoughts. It's something that arises from that potent balancing point between order and chaos, and it usually feels like it comes from somewhere else entirely.

Another definition for an oracle is a *divine messenger*. You've probably run across the term *oracle* if you've spent some time with Greek mythology. Oracles were human intermediates between gods and the public, acting as channels for ethereal wisdom. In modern terms, an oracle can also be a language, system, framework, sacred action, or an object that acts as a channel between you and your magic.

For all intents and purposes, both astrology and tarot can

be oracles. Astrology gives us the framework and language to unearth our magic. Tarot cards include imagery that helps trigger our subconscious and see things from a new, unique perspective so we can access our magic. Those are two of the most well-known oracles, but there are so many more obscure oracles out there that it can sometimes be overwhelming to choose one. These are some of the oracles I've personally worked with and find insightful and empowering.

ORACLE DECKS

When you're browsing the shelves of your local witchy shop or bookstore, you'll probably come across plenty of oracle decks stacked between the tarot decks. As mentioned in the previous chapter, oracle decks can have any number of cards, in any order, with any type of imagery. There are oracle decks that include plants and their metaphysical meaning, phases of the moon, ancient symbology, and just about anything else you can think of.

I like to mix oracle cards in with my tarot readings for a number of reasons. First, it's important to stay open and flexible, and when you've been reading tarot for a while, you can develop a closed view of what the cards mean. Adding in an oracle card or two helps me to see things from a different angle, especially if it's a deck that touches on situations or ideologies that don't show up in traditional tarot interpretations. Because there are usually fewer cards in an oracle deck, they also tend to have a broader meaning. For example, in Kim Krans's *Archetypes* deck, there are cards that represent overarching concepts and archetypes, like the Maiden, the Ocean, and the Sword. Using oracle cards can help to give you a bird's-eye view of a situation and to see a deeper, universal meaning. And, honestly, they're just really fun to look at.

CLEROMANCY

Other oracles include small objects instead of cards, but they still work in a similar way to a tarot or oracle card reading. Cleromancy represents the "casting of lots," or the practice of tossing small charms, tokens, runes, nature objects, or even bones and then reading the patterns they create. Cleromancy is an ancient tool that shows up in one way or another in cultures around the world, although the objects used vary by region. There are also a variety of ways to cast, but most include using a grid or mat that is sectioned off according to areas of your life, such as home, career, or spirituality. Then choose which items to cast and gently toss them onto the grid. I've done this with small jewelry charms that I've assigned my own meanings to and with a grid that I created on my own, but you can also buy cleromancy sets online to use as you see fit.

LITEROMANCY

For creatives who work with words, literomancy can be an especially potent oracle. Literomancy is the art of using words and letters as a channel for magic. It was once especially popular in parts of China, where a single name was written down and analyzed by a literomancer. There are also many different versions of this art, including some modern iterations that involve using song lyrics, poetry, and snippets from newspapers and magazines to help trigger your intuition and hear your inner voice. My favorite version of literomancy is to use the books already on my shelves. I ask a question (similar to a question I might ask my tarot deck) then open any book to a random page. Then I read the page until a phrase or passage stands out to me. I trust that the message behind those words holds the answer I'm looking for.

MEDITATION

In my opinion, this is *the* oracle and the one that gets the least attention. That's because meditation is not flashy. There are no glossy cards or poetic star charts or sparkly crystals. It's not really Instagrammable, and from the outside, it looks like there's not a lot going on. It's also . . . not very fun, especially when you're first starting your practice. It takes a lot of discipline to make yourself slow down and sit long enough to listen, and honestly, being face-to-face with *all* of yourself like that can be really uncomfortable. But for as triggering as meditation can be, it's equally as rewarding.

This sacred discipline can be incredibly powerful on multiple levels. Not only are you sending the message that you are important enough to take a pause each day for no other reason but to listen to your inner wisdom, but there is literally nothing between you and your magic. It's you with you, and that's a beautiful and powerful thing.

SCRYING

If meditation feels too hard, you can always add in special tools and practices to help make it easier. Scrying is an ancient technique that involves meditating while staring at an object. Gazing into a candle flame, bowl of water, or a mirror gives your mind something to focus on so that your inner voice has room to speak. Some scryers see actual visions within the surface they're working with and interpret those images for divination purposes, but truly, it doesn't have to be that intense. Every time I've scryed, the insights I get are mostly internal. They tend to come up as unexpected thoughts and feelings, much like you might get while you're doing a mundane chore or going for a walk.

NATURE WALKS

Speaking of walks, taking a literal hike can also act as an oracle. Some of us find it much easier to access our magic when we keep our bodies moving. Like most oracles, there is variation in how you do this practice, and technically, you can take a walk anywhere while meditating on the sights, sounds, and scents you encounter. Personally, I like to take my meditative walks in the forest. When you first get started, you'll want to give yourself at least ten minutes to settle into the walk. Then, start actively observing your surroundings. As you do, something may stand out to you. It could be a bird, a rock—even something as small and simple as a leaf. Once you find it, stop and spend some time with it. You can describe it in detail in your mind to see if it triggers an insight. You could engage your other senses with the item by touching or smelling it (if it's safe to do so) to see if that spurs an insight. You could also try speaking directly to the object to connect and create a channel with it, which is also a form of animism. I've practiced all these versions of nature walks, and even if I haven't always gotten the answers I seek, the walk alone has acted as a balm to soothe my nervous system so that I was open enough to receive some insight later.

COVENS

It may be strange to think about a coven as an oracle, but when used in a specific way, it definitely can be. In part 1, we discussed how being a part of a group of like-hearted people can be a potent tool in your magic-making toolbox. On top of offering support, and encouraging you to dream bigger, your coven can also act as a channel. I can't tell you how many times I've been talking with my coven about something that's been bothering me, only to have a member say something ridiculously profound that I never would have thought of on my own. I have untangled many personal and creative problems in this way, and the best part is that the person who spits out the wisdom usually doesn't realize just how impactful their words are.

We know from mythology and history that people can be oracles, too. Just like any insight into your magic you receive through an oracle, be sure to double-check it against your own intuition to see if it feels right. If it does, and it's empowering, then go for it! Your magic is yearning to be used. Your boldest creative self has been waiting for you to show up.

You've arrived just in time.

· ·

SPELLWORK: CREATE YOUR OWN ORACLE

Whether you decide to use your own oracle or not is totally up to you, but creating your own out of the things you already have can be an insightful exercise in making magic. For one, it shows you that you don't need special crystals, cards, or trinkets to do this work. Second, crafting your own oracle can help you get used to assigning personal meaning to objects, which is great practice for seeing the connection between your intuition, the stars, cards, and any other oracles you choose to add to your spiritual toolbox.

It's important to note that you absolutely don't have to put together an oracle right this minute if you aren't inspired to. Maybe you'll come back to this section later, or maybe you won't. Another option is to write down your ideas for each of the steps below in your notebook so you have them handy in case you decide to try it.

STEP 1: SET AN INTENTION

Working with any oracle requires that you get clear on what you want from it, but it's doubly important to set an intention when you're creating a tool from scratch. Before you choose your objects, write down your intention for your oracle in your notebook. Maybe you want this oracle to focus on your creativity, or maybe you want it to be extremely blunt and deliver hard truths. Whatever it is, get clear, and write down exactly what you want from it.

STEP 2: FIND YOUR OBJECTS

Start with the things that you already surround yourself with. For example, just looking at my (messy) desk right now, I see a rock from my garden, an amethyst crystal, a charm from my broken brace-let, a seashell, and my daughter's pink flamingo eraser. There's no reason why these items can't be grouped together to create my own version of an oracle. I could use them to do cleromancy readings, or I could consciously choose the one I feel I needed for the day and meditate on it. Consider: What objects do you have access to right now? Or which objects would you like to specifically create or curate to make your oracle?

STEP 3: ASSIGN MEANING

This is the fun part! Now you get to decide what each of your objects means. Using my example, I may choose that pink flamingo eraser as a symbol for play and joy. The broken charm could mean resistance or broken connections. You get the picture. Choose meanings that make sense to you based on how the objects make you feel or what they remind you of. And be sure to keep in mind what your overall intention is for the oracle. If you're creating an oracle that tells hard truths, that flamingo may be a little too soft and sweet with its current meaning.

STEP 4: PRACTICE

The final step is to keep exploring as you practice. Give yourself plenty of readings with your oracle, or try them on someone you trust. You could choose to make a grid, like in cleromancy readings, or skip that part. Play around until you feel like you've built up a solid relationship with it and you feel as though it's a helpful tool on your path to higher creativity.

SPELLWORK: CHECK IN WITH YOUR CREATIVITY TOOLBOX

It's time to flip back through your notebook and check in with the creativity toolbox you started back in part 1. Spend a moment reflecting on the tools you've learned and filling in your chart.

PART III

· ·

THE PROCESS

10

CLEARING THE CHANNEL

∗

NOW THAT YOU have some tools in your toolbox, let's talk about *how* to actually put them to use.

It may seem like it's pretty simple. If you have a hammer, all you have to do is pick it up and swing it, right? But there's a fine art to using a heavy-ended tool like a hammer. You can't swing too softly lest you barely tap the nail into place. And you definitely can't go bananas and bash in your wall, unless that crumbling drywall aesthetic is what you're going for. There's a bit of skill that comes with using your tools if you want to be both efficient and effective.

You've picked out your favorite deck, you've pulled up your natal chart on your phone, and . . . now what? If you take a quick glance at your moon sign and see it's in Gemini, read up that you should socialize with a close group of friends for emotional fulfillment, then leave your creative project in the dust while you scroll through Instagram, you aren't doing yourself any favors. That's pretty much the spiritual equivalent of bashing in your walls.

Before you sit down to use your tools, you have to clear the pathway to your creativity's highest expression. You wouldn't randomly smash holes in your walls; you'd aim for the nail. And that's exactly what we're going to do with your tools— clear everything that's in your way so you can hit the nail on the head. The first time and every time.

WHAT'S A "CHANNEL," ANYWAY?

Just like a *channel* represents a passageway between two larger bodies of water, a channel in more esoteric terms is the passageway between your most brilliant, powerful self and the actual product you make. And what literally stands between the idea and the product?

You. You're the channel.

You're the passage between the ethereal and the physical, between the mystical and the mundane. Going back to the idea of activations in part 1, the act of being a clear channel helps us to reach a state of sacred *connection*. When we participate in this step of the process, we are opening ourselves up to *all* possibilities and can more readily see the connection between our daily lives and the hum of magic just beneath the surface.

Let's go back to that channel metaphor for a second. If we think of a channel as a waterway, then we can assume that the clearer it is, the easier it is for water to flow. Debris of any kind can significantly slow down and even block it.

You don't want trash floating around in your channel, sullying up the water, and blocking your flow. Similarly, you don't want your own psychic mess blocking the essence of your creative idea from getting onto the page. The goal is to try to keep yourself clear—physically, mentally, emotionally, and spiritually—so you can do the work you know in your heart you're meant to do.

The other thing to consider is that if you are working to be clear so you can hear your magic, the tools you use *also* need to be clear. When working with magic-making tools, it's important to "reset" them between uses by removing any energy they may have picked up, taking care of them, and even blessing them.

This may seem like a lot of work, but raw creativity comes with an inherent responsibility. Of course, you should absolutely find joy in your work, but you also have to recognize that if you're creating for public consumption, whether that's a book that will be read by millions or a manuscript for only your closest friends, you have the power to profoundly change someone. As we know, art has power.

What will you do with yours?

CLEARING YOUR TOOLS

There are a lot of different ways to cleanse and purify the tools you're using. I'll go over some of the most popular ways to do so that include sacred plants, herbs, and other ingredients, but please know that they aren't necessary to do this work. You can also clear your tools in a way that doesn't require any extras.

The key to clearing energy from anything—and that includes yourself—is to tap into our four elements again. You can choose to use one element that you identify with most strongly, or all four; it's up to you. I generally clear energy with the air element, but if I inherit something or pull out an old tool that's covered in dust, I tend to use multiple elements to really cleanse it.

Here are some ways to clear your tools with both extra assets and nothing extra at all.

WATER

+ Anoint your tools with floral or distilled water.
+ Rinse them in running water (either your faucet or in nature).
+ Set them near an offering bowl of water.

EARTH

+ Bury them in fresh soil overnight.
+ Create a crystal grid directed at them.
+ Take them on a nature walk with you.

AIR

+ Burn incense and run them through the smoke.
+ Hold them in your hands and let the breeze caress them.
+ Play chimes and other healing sounds in their presence.

FIRE

+ Burn a candle and imagine the flame melting away any energy.
+ Light a match and let the smoke waft over them.
+ Set them out in sunlight for an hour.

CLEARING YOURSELF

Just like we tapped into the elements' wisdom to clear our tools, we'll do the same for ourselves. To get ready to create, we need to clear our physical, emotional, mental, and spiritual "bodies." There are a lot of different names for these different sects of ourselves. In yoga, they're called the *koshas*. In modern mysticism, they're layers of the aura. For clarity purposes, we'll just call them the *bodies*.

Each one requires special care and attention to keep clear, and when they get a little murky, they require their own unique medicine to help them come back to full vibrancy. When all of them are clear and humming along fabulously, it's a million times easier to tune in to your magic (we'll cover that part in the next chapter).

Here are some ways you can clear each of these bodies.

THE PHYSICAL BODY

The physical body is our skin suit that gets us to our desks each morning. It's the vehicle by which we transform an idea into a finished product. It's also all the aches and pains we bring along for the ride with us. The physical body is linked to the earth element, the suit of pentacles, underground root systems, spring, Taurus, Virgo, and Capricorn zodiac signs, Venus, and healing through our five physical senses.

NATURE MAGIC

One of the most potent things you can do to heal your physical body is to honor its cycles and patterns. Understand that growth takes time, and making small, deliberate steps forward is compassionate and sustainable. *Listen* to your physical body in earnest. When it aches, trust that there's a message it's asking you to take notice of. In fact, making space to honor your body's seasons is a potent way to clear it. You could spend ten minutes stretching and listening, completing a grounding yoga sequence with lots of floor poses, or foam rolling.

ELEMENTAL MAGIC

Using assets that literally come from the earth can also be very healing. Plant medicines of all kinds are excellent for grounding and clearing energy. You could fill your home with them, ingest them through teas and fresh foods, or dry and burn herbs. You can also choose a rock or crystal to keep close by while you work, or use it as a "worry stone" when you're thinking through the logistics of any problem. Ritual is also extremely potent in balancing the physical body. Ritual helps ground our physical bodies into the present moment and release stress we may still be carrying from the past. You could create a ritual as simple as clearing your desk each time you sit down to work or something as intricate as a yoga sequence, prayer, meditation, or anything that helps you feel focused and grounded.

ASTROLOGY

Take a look back at your natal chart and find your houses that are ruled by Taurus, Virgo, and Capricorn. Taurus helps us identify what makes us feel secure. Virgo helps us to see what is needed and what is just distraction. Capricorn shows us how to build something of substance from the ground up. If you have planets in these signs, their unique energy can give you a hint as to how to best work with this trio of Earth signs.

If you don't have any planets in these signs, you can still leverage the earth element by looking to Venus in your chart. Venus shows us how we can indulge in earthly pleasures, especially those involving your five senses. You'll want to find this planet in your natal chart and identify which sign it falls under. Read through the meanings of both the planet and the sign for hints about how you can best use Venus's sensual power. Here are some ideas to help you get started, but please know this is not a comprehensive list. There are so many more associations with each sign, but the ones below tend to be pretty accessible.

VENUS: SOME WAYS I TAP INTO MY FIVE PHYSICAL SENSES ARE . . .

Aries: spicy foods, cinnamon, physical challenge
Taurus: emerald green, rose petals, houseplants
Gemini: butterfly trinkets, angel aura quartz, spearmint
Cancer: pearls, ocean sounds, a closed-door sanctuary
Leo: gold, sunstone, written affirmations
Virgo: lavender, moss agate, clean surfaces
Libra: rose quartz, ylang-ylang, violin music
Scorpio: phoenix imagery, mugwort, protective salts
Sagittarius: arrow-shaped trinkets, citrine, basil
Capricorn: sapphire, shoulder massage, art depicting mountains
Aquarius: space sounds, ginkgo biloba, neon colors
Pisces: celestite, yarrow, mermaid trinkets

THE DEEPEST ROOTS
A TAROT SPREAD FOR THE PHYSICAL BODY

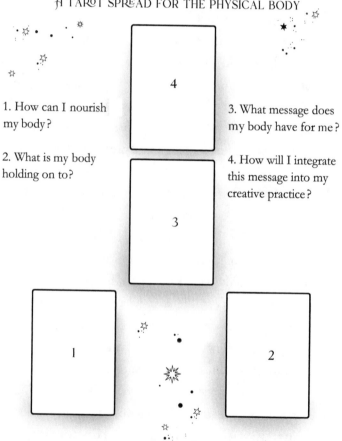

1. How can I nourish my body?

2. What is my body holding on to?

3. What message does my body have for me?

4. How will I integrate this message into my creative practice?

TAROT

For more ideas on clearing the physical body, look to the suit of pentacles, which examines the journey of security and physical resources. You can spend time examining each card's imagery and meaning to generate ideas, or use the specific tarot spread opposite.

THE EMOTIONAL BODY

The emotional body is where we, predictably, store all our emotions. This part of ourselves can get pretty dense, especially when we absorb the emotional experiences of other people. This body is associated with the water element, the suit of cups, rivers, raindrops, bodies of water, winter, Cancer, Scorpio, and Pisces zodiac signs, the moon, and healing through feeling.

NATURE MAGIC

In nature, water acts as both life-giver and preserver. In warmer months, rivers and raindrops nourish all the land so everything can thrive and bloom. In the winter, though, smaller bodies of water freeze over, snow blankets the underbrush, and the world seems to come to a standstill. Nature magic teaches us to allow our emotions to ebb and flow. There's a season for full-bodied emotion, when it's crucial to allow your feelings to flow generously outward, and there's a season to go quiet and listen to the messages they have for you. Create space for this natural rhythm in your day-to-day life. Journaling is a great way to process emotions on the page, and don't discount the power of a good, long cry.

Elemental Magic

Water in all its natural forms is generally soothing, but it can also do wonders to help bring your emotional body into balance. Baths and showers with essential oils are a special kind of magic that can help your physical body relax long enough to allow your emotions to bubble up so you can feel through them. Some other options are to spritz floral waters, like rose and violet water, on your skin and around your work space or drink herbal teas and infused waters. You can also practice tidal wave breathing, which is a yogic breathing technique that involves breathing in through your nose, then slowly pushing air out through your teeth to make a *shhh* sound like an ocean wave.

Astrology

Look at your natal chart for the houses ruled by Cancer, Scorpio, and Pisces—our water sign trio. The houses these signs are located in can give you hints as to how to leverage each sign's unique gifts. Cancer shows us how to create an inner sanctuary. Scorpio helps us access our emotional depth to find our true power. Pisces opens our intuition and helps us see how we're all connected. Any planets you have in these signs can also guide you to accessing your emotional and intuitive depths.

Our moon is also associated with the water element. It follows its own rhythm and ebbs and flows, waxes and wanes each month. There are so many different ways to work with moon magic to clear your emotional body. One potent way is to pay close attention to the moon phases. There are a ton of different apps and websites that can tell you what the moon is up to on any given day. When it's waxing, give yourself the opportunity to outwardly express your feelings, whether that's having a private cry session or telling someone how you feel. When it's waning, draw inward to your journal and meditate.

You can also look specifically at your moon sign to give you an idea for how you can feel it all to heal it all. Here are some ideas for each sign:

THE MOON: I TRANSMUTE EMOTIONS INTO POWER THROUGH . . .

Aries: movement
Taurus: practical tasks
Gemini: conversation
Cancer: memories
Leo: play
Virgo: organizing my surroundings
Libra: listening to others
Scorpio: alone time
Sagittarius: exploration
Capricorn: strategizing what's most important
Aquarius: developing an idea
Pisces: meditation

TAROT

The suit of cups is the suit ruled by water in the tarot. Flip through all ten cards for ideas on how the characters in the tarot story brought their emotional depths to the consciousness so they could end their journey with feelings of hope, love, and fulfillment.

THE CATALYST
A TAROT SPREAD FOR THE EMOTIONAL BODY

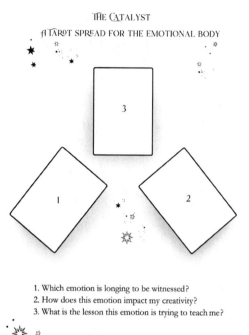

1. Which emotion is longing to be witnessed?
2. How does this emotion impact my creativity?
3. What is the lesson this emotion is trying to teach me?

THE MENTAL BODY

If you're a creative who writes books, poetry, songs, or any number of media that require mental agility with words, your mental body definitely needs some TLC. It can be challenging to discern which voice belongs to *us* and which voice is a conglomeration of our parents, the art teacher who said we'd never do anything great, politicians, newscasters, and even other creatives. Clearing the mental body helps us to hear our inner voice and express it with authenticity. It's associated with the air element, the suit of swords, windstorms and light breezes, autumn, Gemini, Libra, and Aquarius zodiac signs, Mercury, and healing through reprogramming negative thought patterns.

NATURE MAGIC

Although it's invisible, air is incredibly important to a thriving ecosystem. It delivers seeds, scents, and other forms of information from one place to another, helping to both expand understanding and prepare for what's coming. It's always easier to discern which information you need to deal with right *now* when you give your mental body a good scrub-down, and the most effective way to do that is through meditation of any kind. Another great way to clear it is through focused concentration, as it allows all thoughts that aren't related to what you're doing to fall away. Scrying is another tool for focused concentration, as is detailed observation of your environment. Like the leaves in autumn, nature encourages us to let go of the thoughts that we no longer need to hold on to.

ELEMENTAL MAGIC

On top of helping to expand our mental horizons, the air element also teaches us how to be flexible in our thinking. The wind changes direction, and our thought processes can, too, if needed. Chatting with a member of your coven (or your entire coven) at the beginning of the day can help to infuse your process with a fresh perspective, while also offering a bit of accountability. Practicing certain forms of literomancy is another way to clear the mental body. You could pick up a book and choose a phrase, then journal about what that phrase means to you. Or you could choose to journal in general as a way to spill all your thoughts on the page, essentially placing them somewhere outside of your mind for safekeeping. The voice that's left is your true voice. To calm an overactive mind, ujjayi breathing is another excellent tool that can help you release anxiety and worry. To practice, breathe in deeply through the nose until your belly is fully expanded, then release through the nose while allowing the air to move along the back of your throat, making a soft sound as it releases. And if you need a quick air-balancing tool, burning incense is another way to completely and efficiently clear the air.

ASTROLOGY

Time to glance back at your natal chart. This time, find the houses ruled by Gemini, Libra, and Aquarius. Gemini shows us how a variety of viewpoints can fuel our ideas. Libra helps us see ourselves in the other. Aquarius recognizes that most ideas worth pursuing will push others out of their comfort zones. Any planets you have in these signs will help you understand how to leverage the gifts of these signs.

Mercury is considered the "air planet" that most directly impacts us on a day-to-day basis. It rules thinking, listening, communication, and travel—all air-related activities. Not to mention it was named after the messenger of the gods who wore wings on his feet. In our charts, Mercury can show us how to access our truth so we can identify our inner voice.

MERCURY: MY TRUE VOICE SOUNDS LIKE . . .

Aries: short, direct action statements
Taurus: clear and concise sentences
Gemini: curiosity and the urge to find out more
Cancer: emotional connection
Leo: amusement and storytelling
Virgo: focusing on important details

Libra: impartial, nonjudgmental statements
Scorpio: getting straight to the underlying truth
Sagittarius: pep talks and inspirational quotes
Capricorn: distilling expertise into bite-size chunks
Aquarius: innovative ideas and solutions
Pisces: self-talk and daydreams

Tarot

Ruled by the air element, the suit of swords in your deck can help you glean more insight in your own mental body. Because the imagery of this suit tends to be more intense than others, spending extra time examining these cards and observing which thoughts come up can be extremely powerful.

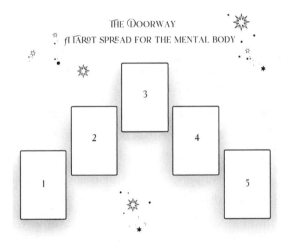

The Doorway
A Tarot Spread for the Mental Body

1. An overview of my project.
2. Which thoughts are blocking me from seeing the whole picture?
3. Which thoughts are needed to elevate my art?
4. Which thoughts am I holding onto that are not mine?
5. How can I release them?

THE SPIRITUAL BODY

Easily the most nebulous of the four, the spiritual body is often hard to define. I think this is because spirituality, and what it means to be in communion with spirit or ether, is so incredibly personal. To get a sense of this body, we look to the fire element. Fire transforms. It's life changing. It has the potential to keep us warm or burn everything to the ground. When we're stuck in our creative process and can't see the big picture, it's often because some part of us is afraid to light the match. On top of fire, the spiritual body is also associated with the suit of wands, lightning, wildfires, summer, Aries, Leo, and Sagittarius zodiac signs, Mars and the sun, and healing through aligned action.

NATURE MAGIC

We rise and slumber by the rhythm of our sun. It's the source of our vitality and the luminary by which our entire solar system orbits. We can't talk about clearing our spiritual bodies without making space for the things that light us up, the things that we would center all of our days around if we could. Think about what that could be in your own life. If it happens to be your creative project (which it often is), you want to make time to actually *work on* it in earnest. I know that seems pretty obvious, but there are so many creatives who long to work on their projects, but don't for one reason or another. The warmth of loving what you love and giving yourself space for it is one of the most effective ways to connect with your spiritual body. Embrace the sun and all its gifts, just like we do in summer.

ELEMENTAL MAGIC

Fire can be dangerous if we don't take proper safety measures. When working with fire in elemental magic, it's important to create a safe space, or vessel, before you begin. For many of us, a safe space may look like a coven or community that is carefully curated so that it fans the flames of our inspiration instead of putting them out. It could be a fan fiction forum, dance squad, or a text thread with your closest friends. We can take the concept of acting from our hearts literally and engage in any activities that elevate our heart rates. Things that bring you joy and incorporate play also help to clear the spiritual body. If you want to work with literal fire, you can always set an intention for healing and clearing by carving into a candle and then lighting it, or write down anything that's holding you back from your highest self, then burn it.

ASTROLOGY

Find the houses in your chart that are ruled by Aries, Leo, and Sagittarius. Aries shows us how to access our courage. Leo encourages us to act from the heart. Sagittarius guides us to expand our horizons to find our spiritual truth. Pay extra attention to any planets in these signs, as they can deliver information about your own unique fire power.

You also want to take a closer look at Mars in your chart. This is our personal planet of aggression and willpower, but when it's working to its highest potential, Mars shows us how we take *aligned action*. We aren't talking about action just because we feel like we should be doing something but action that's in harmony with what our spirit wants to express through us.

Mars: I move closer to what lights me up by . . .

Aries: challenging myself
Taurus: indulging in my physical senses
Gemini: following my urge for novelty
Cancer: forging tight emotional bonds
Leo: asserting my power
Virgo: finding a solution to a problem
Libra: creating something beautiful
Scorpio: going all in on something
Sagittarius: the freedom to explore
Capricorn: building something that will last
Aquarius: experimenting and testing hypotheses
Pisces: acting on my intuitive voice

Tarot

Take a look through the suit of wands in your tarot deck. Similar to the swords, the journey does not end with rainbow skies and smiling children. The Ten of Wands depicts a person overburdened with responsibility; they're able to complete the journey, but not without stifling some of their creative fire. Which concepts and supports can you take from the suit of wands, and which should you leave behind so as not to take on too much?

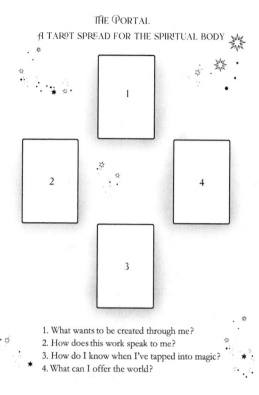

THE PORTAL
A TAROT SPREAD FOR THE SPIRITUAL BODY

1. What wants to be created through me?
2. How does this work speak to me?
3. How do I know when I've tapped into magic?
4. What can I offer the world?

SPELLWORK: CREATE YOUR CLEARING RITUALS

Clearing all these bodies can seem extremely overwhelming, especially when you're already short on time to create. But trust me when I say this: Taking a few moments to clear your energy bodies and your tools before you work makes all the difference. Even if you aren't sure *why* it makes a difference, just the habit of performing a ritual helps to prepare all the parts of you to create. It's easier to get started from this state of readiness instead of discord and stress.

CURATE YOUR IDEAL RITUAL

Grab your notebook and look back over this chapter. Imagine you have all the time you need to do a ritual before you create. Choose at least one item or action from all the suggestions for each of the bodies to include in your ritual. You can also mix and match these, as in a yoga flow for the physical body, tapping into the moon phase for the emotional body, meditation for the mental body, and lighting a candle for the spiritual body. Also, be sure to consider the gifts that the moon, Mercury, Venus, and Mars have to offer and what you could add to your ritual to access their energy. Write down your ideal ritual in your notebook.

CURATE YOUR EXTRA CLEANSING RITUAL

If it's been a while since you've done a ritual, or you've been through a really intense time in your life, you may want to spend some extra time clearing the bodies. You can do this anytime you feel like it or your intuition is nudging you to do so.

Again, go back through all of the items and actions that help clear the channel. Choose things that may require more time and depth, or multiple options for each of the bodies. This will be the ritual you use when you feel like you need an extra-deep energy cleansing.

CURATE YOUR MINI RITUAL

Life comes at you fast, and sometimes, you're squeezing creativity into small pockets of time. For these situations, you also want to make a mini ritual. Think: a ritual that quickly clears all the bodies in ten minutes or less. My mini ritual usually involves a quick yoga stretch, spritzing some floral water, lighting incense and then the candle on my desk. I finish it off by setting an intention to be a clear channel while I work. You can borrow my ritual or create your own mini ritual by using the four element power items you identified at the end of "The Elements" chapter.

11

TUNING IN

ONCE WE'VE CLEARED our energetic bodies and cleansed our sacred tools, we're ready to tune in to our magic and the creative power it has to offer us.

First, let's talk about what I mean by *tuning in*. The process is similar to fiddling with the tuning knob on a car radio. You may be operating at your regular frequency as you go about your everyday life, but when you sit down to create, you need to work from a higher frequency to be able to hear your magic and tap into the fullest extent of your creative power. That requires you to tweak the knob, millimeter by millimeter, until you can hear the tone and feel the texture of your magic. Clearing the channel before you tune in helps to erase the static from the airwaves so you can find it faster.

As you commit yourself to this process and become more familiar with your magic, you could hop right into tuning in and skip your clearing rituals. In fact, it's likely that your magic will start to communicate with you at random times— even when you aren't actively creating—as you interact with it regularly. It also stands to reason that if you're engaging in clearing rituals regularly, your energetic bodies will continue to be in pretty good shape. All this to say, I still do some version of my ritual just about every time I sit down to write. I find the process instantly grounding, and even after years of practice, it still helps to block out the static.

Intuition is a relationship between you and the universe, as told through the language of your personal brand of magic. Taking steps to tune in to and listen to your magic can help you to create with less friction (and honestly, save you some heartache in the process). Going back to our activations, it's our *highest creativity* that we experience when we tune in.

Creativity in its most spiritual form opens all kinds of doors that we didn't even realize were possible. We see our work from different angles. Once-insurmountable problems seem to gracefully come undone when we see them from a different perspective. We may try things we never dreamed of, only to find that they lead us on a much more satisfying and successful path. When our highest creativity is activated, it's almost guaranteed that the path to our dreams won't look the way we envisioned. It'll be surprising, and thrilling, and a tad bit scary, but it *should* be. We're finally creating to our fullest potential.

The truth is that if you do the same things you've always done, you're going to get what you've always gotten. Tuning in will take us off-roading into unknown territory.

And that's a beautiful thing.

PROTECTION

There are a lot of different viewpoints among modern mystics when it comes to protecting yourself while you're tuning in. For every theory about ghosts, demons, and evil entities out there, there's a modern mystic that doesn't entertain those beliefs at all. I've studied with teachers and mystics that run the full spectrum from skeptics to psychic mediums who communicate with the dead, and most agree that some form of protection is essential when tuning in to higher frequencies.

I'm not fluent in ghosts, so I can't tell you if protection really is essential. What I can tell you is that I do it anyway, mostly because it can't hurt. If anything, doing a physical act to declare your boundaries or setting an intention as you tune in will only help you get extra clear on what you want to receive (and what you don't).

Some options for setting boundaries include pouring salt across the threshold to your work area, setting dark-colored crystals in all four corners of your room, or doing a short meditation where you visualize yourself and your work space surrounded by a bubble of white light. You can also just keep it simple and set a verbal intention. Usually I'll say something like, "I only allow insights and information that's for my highest good and the highest good of all."

OFFERINGS

Now that you're officially ready to tune in, we'll start with an offering. This isn't some strange cultlike offering, I promise. No blood sacrifices required.

Since we're activating your highest creative potential, and the person who confidently works from that space regularly, we're going to make an offering to your future self. And the best part? You can choose anything you want to offer up.

Choosing an offering is individual to each and every creative. Some creatives I know choose a tarot card with imagery that represents their dreams. Others offer crystals, flowers, small charms or trinkets, or imagery and items associated with certain planets and zodiac signs. You can also choose whether to use the same offering for multiple sessions in a row or to change it up each time you sit down to create.

It can be a lot of fun to experiment with different items to use for your offering, but when in doubt, you can always offer up your most potent asset: your creativity. I usually make a small offering of a crystal, a tarot card, and some other related trinkets, and I include a snippet from something I'm writing. Sometimes, it's a line directly from my manuscript, and other times, it's a secret hope or wish from my journal. If you're a visual artist, you could offer something as small as a doodle or as big as a completed canvas. You get the picture.

By making an offering to your future self, no matter how big or small, you're acting in good faith that this powerful, magical version of you exists on some time line. And this future you is fluent in magic. Your offerings are the bridge that will take you from apprentice to alchemist, from the Fool to the World.

SUPPORTS

You also want to check to be sure you have the supports you need for the creative session you're about to embark on. Supports can be anything from your frankincense essential oil to your lower-back support pillow. Any of your assets and tools can fill the role of support as you see fit.

When I was drafting this book, I leaned heavily on supports that help ground me and keep me clearheaded. For me, that meant draping the same blanket on my lap before each writing session for comfort and familiarity. I also used a mint-scented essential oil to promote clarity. I rubbed a few drops on my throat to symbolize precision in my writing. On days when I felt especially overwhelmed by the task at hand, I pulled out the Star card from my favorite tarot deck and propped it up near my keyboard. It served as a visual reminder to reconnect with my magical future self—the one who had already written her heart out and finished this book—whenever I got scared.

What about you? What supports do you need for your next creative session? The wonderful thing about sacred tools is that they can be used in multiple ways—for clearing, communication, self-discovery, support, and more. You get to decide how they would best serve you in any given situation, and that role is always subject to change.

If you aren't sure exactly what you need, you can always go back to the bodies. Does your physical body have what it needs to feel supported? Emotional, mental, and spiritual bodies? Answer those questions and go from there.

LISTEN AND REALIGN

Before you pick up that paintbrush or tap the first letter on your keyboard, take a deep breath. You've set yourself up for success in every way you possibly can, and that is the part of learning your magic that you can control. From this point forward in the creative process, it's the magic that's running the show, and you're along for the ride.

Give yourself a second to settle into your work space. Check in with yourself: Are you ready to go? If the answer is yes, it's time to get started. If you still feel like something is off, ask your future self what you still need. Just be extremely cautious here. Sometimes, it's easier to do all the prep work than it is to actually sit down and create, and I've witnessed many creatives get caught up in making sure that everything is flawless before they begin. That's not the point of tuning in.

Remember: We're simply turning the knob until we contact the magic. There will always be some static in the background. There will always be a chance that the sound may cut out, or that it will be a little warbled, or even that it won't be your favorite song playing, but you'll like it enough for the moment. Perfection is a construct—it's not real. Nothing is perfect, and this process won't be, either. If something feels genuinely off, readjust and realign. Otherwise, trust yourself and trust the process.

· ·

SPELLWORK: CREATE YOUR OFFERINGS AND SUPPORTS

At this point, it probably seems like it'll be a million years before you get to actually creating. I promise you, though, that these steps can be as quick and simple as you want them to be. In fact, most days, I use the same offerings and supports, and they're already on my desk, ready to go. Instead of gathering new items every day, I usually just spend a few minutes reconnecting with my future self and expressing gratitude to her for being with me on my creative journey. I then give a little shout-out to my supports for helping me, and that's pretty much it. Five minutes, tops.

To get started, think of what you'd like your main offering to be. I usually choose one to three items that represent the project I'm currently working on, and I keep them as my offerings until I'm finished with it. Remember, you can use anything you want: specific tarot cards, crystals, symbols, art, and more. Write down some ideas in your notebook.

Once you have that down, consider how you can support yourself while you work on this project. No matter how many books I write, there is always something that scares me a little, whether I'm worried that my skill level isn't up to par for the task at hand, or I'm crunched for time, or something else entirely. Sit with those uncomfortable feelings and think about how you can support yourself through them. Like I mentioned, I incorporated a lot of grounding, earthy supports to help me stay calm and focused while drafting this book, but my supports change with each project. What can you use to physically, emotionally, mentally, and spiritually support yourself? Again, write down all your ideas in your notebook and start to think about anything you need to gather.

12

TAKING THE JOURNEY

THIS IS IT. You've finally arrived at the part where you go all in on your creativity. You're clear, you're tuned in, you're settled at your work space, and now it's time to get to it. If anything, this is the part you *know* how to do.

If you find that the method by which you create is soulful, fulfilling, and leaves you feeling confident and reenergized, please feel free to skip right over this chapter. But if you feel like you're missing something or you're curious as to how to make your own process feel better while creating more aligned art, hang with me for a while.

Just like the tools we've discussed have their own unique language, they also depict the creative journey in their own way. They all reflect the process of moving from the first seed of an idea to a completed project, but each tool abides by its own cycle, pattern, and rhythm. Similarly, all creatives are acting to bring something from idea to finished project, but we each do so according to our own internal wisdom. That's why it's so important to take any creative advice you read with a grain of salt (this book included!). Experimenting with and taking pieces from methods that have worked for others is great. Strictly adhering to them even when they don't totally work for you isn't in your best interest.

Going back to our activations, taking the journey is aligned with *community* in its purest form. To be in community means to *be in communion with.* We know by now that we need the support of others to do this work, but we are also part of our ecosystem and solar system. We are in communion with all of the creatives and magic-makers that have walked before us as we embody universal archetypes and embrace ancient storytelling. Our community expands well outside of our immediate group of friends—it's the trees, the stars, the path already walked by others, and the paths yet to be discovered.

In this chapter, we'll go over some of the paths and patterns that nature, astrology, and tarot show us how to traverse. Each one is unique, but they all take us through the creative journey, from beginning to end, in their own way. You may find you identify with one right away, or you may feel like none of them are exactly what you're looking for. That's okay. Keep an open, curious mind as you review these methods for taking your journey, and consider how they might reflect your own path.

GETTING STARTED

You're already tuned in to your magic, so the very first thing to do is to listen. As you open your electronic file or set up your supplies, get quiet and pay extra-close attention to any insights, nudges, or urges that come up. Approach them with curiosity instead of shutting them down right away. In your notebook, jot down anything interesting that comes up.

In all the following creative journey archetypes, you'll find there are periods of outward action and periods of pause and integration. Ancient mystics and pattern-readers understood the importance of the sacred pause, and that wisdom still holds true today. We can't be effective communicators without also listening. Pause periods are designed to help us rest, reset, review where we've come from so far, and listen to our magic for clues about where we're going.

Keep your notebook close by through the entire process—while you're in a pause period *and* actively creating. Your magic can and is speaking to you at all times, and you may find it gets even louder while you're in the middle of making. Whenever a new insight about your project or process comes up, simply write it down and move on. You can examine it all later.

Each of the following journeys has its own pattern and cadence. Look through to see which one resonates with you, if any. You can adopt one of these journeys for the project you're working on to help build a structure around your natural creative ebbs and flows, or you can choose to set up your next project with one of these journeys in mind. You may choose not to use any at all. The goal is to feel that you're taking aligned action and making forward movement in your creativity sessions. These journey archetypes can help, but they're by no means necessary.

THE MINOR ARCANA JOURNEY

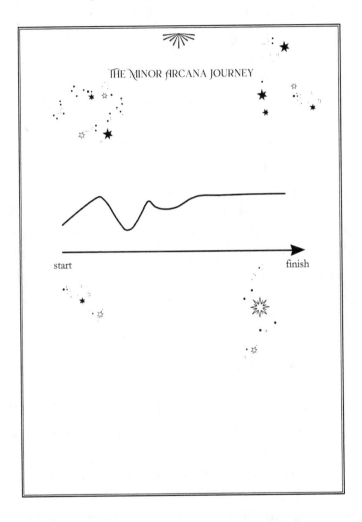

THE MINOR ARCANA JOURNEY

start   finish

In the Minor Arcana, we begin with only the seed of something—as depicted by the ace—and journey through many ups and downs before we reach the final conclusion. It doesn't matter if we're talking about wands, cups, pentacles, or swords—the numbered cards in each suit depict a similar journey from beginning to end.

This creative path is not straightforward (but, honestly, which path worth pursuing is?). It starts with a slow and steady ramp-up as you research and gather all the resources you need to really get going. And just when you're ready to take off . . . it's time for a pause. The fives in each suit denote a setback of some kind. In regard to your creative process, it's a conscious pause that you purposely take. During your pause, you spend time listening to your magic, journaling, meditating, and getting all your resources and research in order before you take flight. When you're ready, you dive all the way into your project, picking up speed at a steady pace, until you reach your second pause right before the finish line. Again, you listen to your magic, recalibrate, and steady yourself for the final push. Then it's all systems go until you cross the finish line.

This action plan may be for you if:

+ You prefer an incremental pace.
+ You like to add on to your daily creative goals a little at a time.
+ You identify with the need to pause and reflect before you take the next leap.
+ You want to practice listening to your magic and building in rest periods.

THE SOLAR JOURNEY

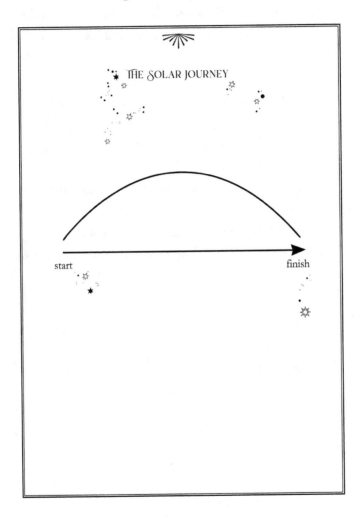

Every morning, our source of light and heat crests the horizon, rises steadily into the sky, then descends at the same cadence until it dips below the surface, signaling the end of our day. When working with a sun-inspired creative journey, a similar pattern emerges. Each day, or each time we sit down to create, we begin by "warming up," increasing our proficiency until we hit the midpoint of our session. Then we begin to cool down through the second half of our session until it's time to finish for the day.

THIS ACTION PLAN MAY BE FOR YOU IF:

+ You prefer consistency and like knowing what to expect.
+ You tend to peak in productivity in the middle of a session.
+ You feel soothed by reliable, consistent effort.
+ You work in shorter bursts and rest fully between sessions.

THE LUNAR JOURNEY

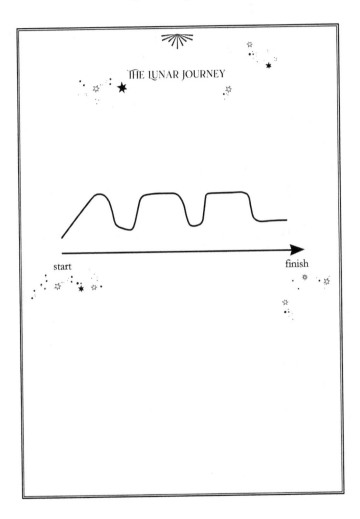

THE LUNAR JOURNEY

start

finish

Our moon also has its own pattern and cadence. Unlike our sun, the moon takes almost an entire month to complete its cycle, from new moon to full moon and then back to new moon again. The sun also appears mostly unchangeable in the sky, whereas our moon often wears a different face. Sometimes, it shines brightly, demanding our fullest attention, and other times, it disappears altogether.

The lunar journey is more fluid and changeable, yet it still guides us to a satisfying finish to our most cherished projects. Creatives who take this path don't cycle through prep work, creating, and organizing all in one session, for every session, like they do on a solar journey. Instead, they tend to spend a couple of days preparing, a couple of days actively creating, a couple of days organizing and cleaning up, and a couple of days resting and listening before they start all over again.

THIS ACTION PLAN MAY BE FOR YOU IF:

+ You prefer to finish one whole section of a large project at a time before moving on to another section.
+ You need a little flexibility, or you'll get bored.
+ You crave short periods of time to fully recharge in the midst of a big project.
+ You like the idea of working with smaller cycles and actions to keep yourself on track.

THE SEASONAL JOURNEY

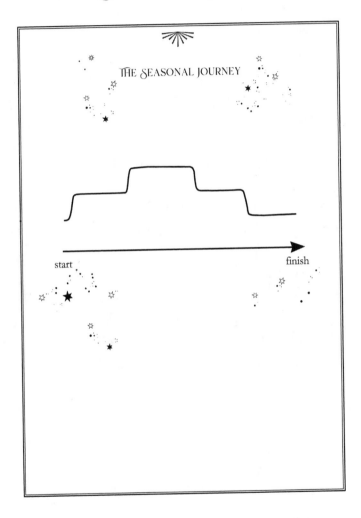

Nature's seasons show us how rewarding it can be to settle into a season for a good, long while. There's something deeply humbling about acquiescing to the gifts and difficulties of each season, whether that's the isolation of winter or the pressure to blossom in summer. There are only four seasons, and each one stretches on for months, requiring us to become masters of one part of our craft before moving on to the next. Each season is a long haul, which means that you could be preparing and researching for months, then actively creating for months, and *then* revising and reworking for months before you finally arrive at your period of deep rest.

THIS ACTION PLAN MAY BE FOR YOU IF:

+ You prefer depth over breadth.
+ You don't mind if you spend a long time (think: months) prepping, creating, revising, and then reflecting.
+ You feel confident in your endurance.
+ You know how to rest deeply and for a long time without itching to pick up a new project.

THE RETROGRADE JOURNEY

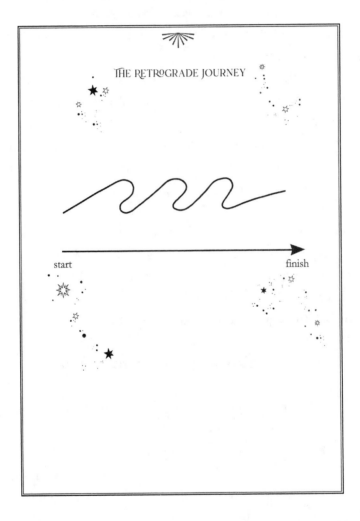

All the planets in our solar system have a retrograde period, where they appear to move backward on their ellipses from our viewpoint on Earth. The length of the retrograde period depends on the planet's distance from us, and each planet has its own rhythm for when it goes retrograde. For example, Mercury appears to move backward through the sky three to four times per year, for about three weeks each time, while Pluto goes retrograde for about five months only once per calendar year.

Even though these planets appear to take a few strides back every once in a while, they still push forward most of the time. And in astrology, retrograde periods are considered highly auspicious times where we can glean insight and wisdom by retracing our steps and thinking about our creativity from an opposing view. In this journey, you move along at a steady pace until you pause, then backpedal. One way this could look would be to write the first act of your screenplay, then going back and rewriting or revising it before moving on to the next act. Anytime you stop forward movement and reverse course, you're following a retrograde-inspired journey.

THIS ACTION PLAN MAY BE FOR YOU IF:

+ You feel comfortable reworking parts of your project before you finish it.
+ The idea of revising or reworking the entire project feels overwhelming; you'd rather do it in chunks, even if that means it'll take you longer to complete the whole thing.
+ You don't have a timeline of when you'd like to finish.
+ You hear your inner voice clearly when you work through what you've already created.

• •

Spellwork: Pick Your Path

Which of these action plans seems most like you? Choose which one you feel most connected to, and consider the following questions:

✦ *Is this action plan working for my current project?*
✦ *Does this action plan feel good?*
✦ *What does rest and listening look like for me with this action plan?*

Write down your answers in your notebook. Remember: You can choose a new path at any point if the one you're currently on isn't working for you. You can switch paths in the middle of a project, between projects, or you could travel the same path for every single creation. You can also blend paths or make up your own.

The point is: Just keep moving forward.

This journey is yours to claim.

13

Distilling the Wisdom

EVENTUALLY, ONE DAY, you're going to finish that project.

It may seem like a pipe dream at this point in your journey, but it's going to happen. You'll write "The End" on your manuscript. You'll spray a coat of sealant on your pottery. You'll hit "publish" on your first blog post.

And then what?

I've asked this question to tons of creatives, and each one has had a different answer. There are creatives who are ready to jump into the next project within the hour and others who tell me they're going to nap into the new year. Most fall somewhere in between, typically saying that they'll take a couple of weeks off before starting the journey all over again.

There's no wrong way to rest between journeys. But to distill the wisdom we've earned on this path, we have to consciously integrate it into our practice. That process looks a bit different from sleeping in and marathoning reality TV, yet it's so incredibly important to the evolution of our magic.

Don't get me wrong, I *love* a good reality TV marathon after a long slog with a manuscript, but I've come to accept it for what it is: recovery. This period of shutting down is a necessary part of coming back into equilibrium after pushing so much of our energy into our creation. When we're in recovery mode, we're mostly unconscious, meaning we've taken our intuition off line for the moment while we indulge our physical senses and earthly pleasures. We aren't thinking about connecting with our future selves, or how to keep our energetic bodies clear, or the messages our tarot cards have for us, or engaging with our magic at all. We only care about when that pizza is going to get here and if we have time to start another movie. There's nothing wrong with this—it's all part of the resting and healing process—but it isn't the only part.

Distilling wisdom requires us to be fully conscious, which means we probably aren't ready to do it the second we finish a project. It takes some time to bring ourselves back on line, but eventually, we get there. We start to feel more like ourselves. Ideas for the next thing begin to poke their way into our minds, and the itch to get back to the drawing board grows more urgent. And this is when a lot of us make a misstep. We head back in before we figure out what we've learned. And more critically, we begin our next journey before we've fully claimed our power.

Power is our secret activation, the one that has the potential to change the world for the better when placed in the right hands. The only way we come into authentic power— the kind that births bold, world-shifting creations with confidence—is by applying hard-earned wisdom to our journey again and again. That means looking at the hard stuff, the ugly stuff, the things that scare us in the light of day. It means zooming in on the less glamorous parts of the process and condensing what you've learned about yourself, your magic, the world, and the universe into something you can take with you in your rucksack on your next adventure. In this way, we become master alchemists, blending tools and time, magic and wisdom, to create powerful, beautiful things that make a profound impact.

A sacred pause is required to claim our power. It's not the most fun part of the creative process, and it definitely doesn't feel very productive, but it's actually the most efficient way to create the kind of art you've always wanted to make. There's no reason to put yourself through the same iteration of the creative journey over and over again when you can take the pause, distill the wisdom, and move on to bigger and bolder things.

Wisdom Through the Wound

It's no secret that pain can be a profound teacher. Most esoteric teachings reference pain as a release point, a soft spot in an otherwise hard shell that allows us to see what's really under there. It's also true that we all experience it. There's no getting around painful experiences in this very human life.

In astrology, the comet Chiron represents both our wound and the wisdom that can be extracted from it. It also separates the visible planets from the invisible ones as it orbits between Saturn and Uranus. Chiron is considered the bridge between our personal experience on Earth and our role in the collective. Think about that: *Our wound* is the bridge between our personal experience and the wisdom we share with others.

Tarot also has its own version of triumph after pain. In the Major Arcana, the Devil depicts us at our most human—chained to the material world and unable to see past our own pain. But then everything that's inconsequential falls away with the Tower, and the Star shows up to guide us. The person in that card has one foot on Earth and one in the water, demonstrating how we're now ready to step into a different role. It's time to consider how we can make a ripple in the collective consciousness.

Pain in all its forms is an entry point to wisdom. When it's time, start by sitting with your most recently completed creative journey. Replay it in your mind from the seed of the idea to your final session. Which parts hurt the most? Where did you feel achy, or awkward, or weak? You can also zoom in on the project itself. Which parts of it explored pain? And what does your creation have to say about pain?

This is the part of the creative process where I have to let you wander a bit on your own, although I'd love to guide you through this every step of the way. The truth is, I can only take you to this sacred threshold and not a step further. The process of distilling your experience into wisdom is deeply personal. Some of us will journal about it. Others will find that too raw and will write a story around it instead. Some of us will work it out through exercise, others will talk it out with their best friend, and others still will find meaning in meditation. More of us will find it through tears.

Here's how you know when you've found it.

You can condense it to a single sentence.

When you can say that silence is the vehicle of creativity, or that grief can grow something beautiful, or that the love is in the commitment (as you've heard me say throughout this book), or anything else that you come up with, you've found it. And now you can apply it to your next journey. It becomes another sacred tool in your toolbox.

This is uncomfortable work, but it's the kind of work that will change you forever. It's in this liminal space that the universe reorganizes itself around us, adjusting to our newfound wisdom and what that means for your future self who's just waiting for you to catch up. It's in this pause that you're learning how to become that version of you.

This is how you prepare your heart to take the leap all over again.

SPELLWORK: THE TEXTURE OF MAGIC

For your final spellwork, we revisit the texture of your personal brand of magic. At the start of this book, we explored what your magic feels like in your body and how your physical senses can act as triggers to help you identify it.

But you know your own magic better now.

You know how to access it with your tools, what it acts and feels like when you're creating, and how to pause to listen to it. Now we don't need to rely on our physical senses so heavily to tap into it.

One last time, I'll ask: What does your magic feel like?

Let your physical senses drop away. Try to answer without them.

What does it feel like?

Spend a moment meditating on this prompt or brainstorming in the notebook that's seen you through this entire process. If you don't come up with something right away, that's okay. You're giving that wisdom space to bubble to the surface in its own time.

And luckily, you know exactly how to do that now.

14

YOU ARE MAGIC

AND SO IS EVERYONE ELSE

THERE ARE A lot of things we still don't know about the universe, but one thing's for sure: our concept of what it means to be a part of the human experience on this rock floating through space will continue to expand.

In the last decade alone, we've made collective strides toward justice and equality and have begun to tear down walls that have held marginalized communities back for far too long. We've also taken quite a few heartbreaking steps back. This is, quite honestly, an extremely difficult time to live through, and with the gap between the rich and poor growing wider and a planet in crisis, it's not about to be a good time.

This is why it's more important than ever to create.

Making art is not above the fight for a freer, fairer world. Art is a *part* of the fight. And when we create it in conversation with magic and empathy and power, it becomes a vehicle for change. It pushes us forward as a society.

On a personal level, when you learn to work in harmony with your magic, you become an example for others. You show them what's possible, and your light serves as a guide for anyone who's ready to pick up their torch and start their own journey. We've talked a lot about magic from a personal perspective in this book, but only so that you fully understand how to apply it so that you can be of service. The fullest expression of your magical, radical, creative self is exactly what we need at this moment in history.

Don't be afraid to make this book your own. Take it apart and stitch the pieces back together in a way that makes sense to you. Whatever it takes to access your magic, do that. These sacred tools and languages have survived for thousands of years *because* they were designed to evolve as we do. Now let them serve you as you evolve so that you can serve others.

Everyone deserves to feel their own magic, to wield their own power. If you are one of the few who found your way to this book and learn how to do so, it's your responsibility to do whatever you can to help others along your journey. With great power comes great responsibility and all that.

There's a lot of work to do on this planet, but the more magic-makers unleashed, the better off we are.

You can do this.

We can do this.

For all of us.

ACKNOWLEDGMENTS

It's hilariously ironic that when I sat down to type out the first words of this book, I froze. This was, after all, the book I'd described to my publisher as a culmination of my life's work, and now that I was under contract for it, I had a hard deadline to make it appear on the page. No pressure, right?

In the end, what got me back to my desk was remembering the very beginning. The first online class I'd ever taught was on the creativity cycle and all its phases, and it's the cornerstone of my philosophy on life in general: Everything is cyclical. An endpoint is really just another beginning in disguise. This book may be a culmination, a full moon phase of *this* part of my work, but it's not the only thing I'll do or the last thing I'll make. It can't be. I'd like to honor this cycle, this book, by thanking all of the people, teachings, and experiences that came into each phase of my life at exactly the right time.

At the new moon phase, my mother's lineage taught about creative joy, openness, and curiosity. Thank you to my mom, Debi, and my grandma, Eleanor, in particular for those lessons. My father's lineage emphasized the importance of structure and focus. Dad, I know you don't get half of the stuff in this book, but you taught me the value of careful study and that anything worth doing is worth doing well. I hope that respect and precision are reflected in these pages.

At the waxing crescent phase, as the light of this work began to make itself known, my high school best friend, Keri, encouraged me to keep going, to keep learning, and was the first person to tell me I'm good at this. Keri, without you, I wouldn't be doing this work. My longtime partner, Matt, has continued to cheer me on, give me space, and listen intently as I spitball about the universe from the very beginning. I love you both endlessly. My many mentors, guides, and teachers along this path, including my spiritual mentor, Robin, and my yoga mentor, Léah, have continued to challenge me, push me, and lovingly showed me the way back to myself, time and time again.

The first quarter phase, a huge turning point: I brought my work online and it changed my life. To everyone in *Unearthed*, but especially the first crew of seventeen that weathered the pandemic together: Heidi, Becca, Aimée, Naomi, Erica, Bri, Patricia, Jess, Megan, Koren, Chris, Alex, Natalie, Tess, Marissa, and both Sarahs. Thank you for riding this out with me while I worked out the kinks. To the students who came after: Thank you for reinforcing that no one owns Jupiter and for having my back. And to my clients: I love doing cosmic therapy with you.

At the waxing gibbous phase, the light expands, and this work found a place in publishing. To my incomparable editor and friend, Mara: There is literally no one else that gets this book like you do. I am so, so grateful. To my entire team at Macmillan, thank you for seeing the potential in me and these pages. And to my agent and ride-or-die, Victoria: I got you to let me read your chart. Maybe I can read your cards next?

Finally, the full moon phase—a culmination and a release. This is where you come in, sweet reader. This work is yours now. In the second half of the cycle, as my personal investment ebbs from this book and the light disseminates, I hope that this work will continue to find its way into creatives' hands. I hope that you continue to find comfort and inspiration here when you need it most.

As for me, it's time to step over the threshold into a new cycle. I hope we'll continue to cross paths on the next journey, magic maker. Here's my final piece of advice: When you feel the urge to rag on Geminis, just remember that one wrote this book. We contain multitudes.

ABOUT THE AUTHOR

Andrea Hannah is an author, astrologer, and workshop leader. She teaches creatives all over the globe and writes about everything from fierce modern fairy tales to the cosmos (she's a Gemini). Her work has appeared in *Bustle, Elite Daily, Thrive Global, HuffPost, Mslexia,* and more.